GETTING AWAY

An interview with Simon Bennett

Was writing for the theatre something you always wanted to do?

No. It was film that always interested me when I was younger. I didn't see my first play until I was twenty-three, *The Trial* at the National Theatre. I used to feel a bit alienated by the theatre - I didn't think theatre people would be interested in me and the things I wrote about. I've changed my mind about that now. I enjoy writing for theatre.

What started you writing?

When I first went to prison me and a mate started rewriting the words to a Tracy Chapman song, just to pass time more than anything, but I found myself enjoying it. I then started writing poetry and short stories, which were picked up on by an English teacher who encouraged me to continue after my release. Which I did. Lovely woman she was.

Were there any writers you studied who had a particular influence on you?

When I read it's mostly novels. Though I did study Osborne and Pinter in a theatre studies group and I have enjoyed reading most of their stuff since. I could name a lot of writers whose work I've enjoyed, but I don't know how much I'm influenced by them, though I'm sure I have been.

I'm not interested in supplying the audience with a particular message, my first objective is to write drama

Simon Bennett
Photo by Charlie Crane

When you begin drafting a play, do you start out with a particular agenda or message that you want to get across?

When I wrote poetry, a lot of my work attacked society and my circumstances but over time I became less interested in that. These days I'm not interested in supplying the audience with a particular message, my first objective is to write drama. Let people analyse it how they want.

You have been very involved with the rehearsal process for Drummers; how have you found it?

To have your play produced at all is good, so to have it directed by Max Stafford-Clark is a real privilege. I really enjoy rehearsals - I find that Max is good at opening up meanings in the writing that I had never thought of. These discoveries sometimes mean I have to rewrite or develop parts of the play which can be hard, but I'm not as protective about my writing as some playwrights. I've also enjoyed making suggestions about how the play should actually be directed, and Max encourages me to do this. I would really like to do some directing in the future.

I suppose that writing or watching a play and going out to the country thieving are both kind of escapist

Simon Bennett and Max Stafford-Clark
Photo by Charlie Crane

Out of Joint,
in association with Karl Sydow, Ambassador Theatre Group,
Cambridge Arts Theatre and Mercury Theatre, Colchester,
presents

BY SIMON BENNETT

This production was first performed at Cambridge Arts Theatre 4 August 1999

First performed at the Traverse Theatre, Edinburgh 12 August 1999

First performed in London at the New Ambassadors Theatre 1 September 1999

Out of Joint registered charity no 1033059

Funded by
THE
ARTS
COUNCIL
OF ENGLAND

The
British
Council

1999 TOUR

4 - 7 August
Cambridge Arts Theatre
01223 503333

12 - 29 August
Traverse Theatre
Edinburgh
0131 228 1404

1 September - 9 October
New Ambassadors Theatre
London
0171 836 6111

13 - 16 October
Mercury Theatre
Colchester
01206 573948

19 - 23 October
Everyman Theatre
Liverpool
0151 709 4776

2 - 6 November
The Drum
Plymouth Theatre Royal
01752 267222

9 - 13 November
Oxford Playhouse
01865 798600

Do you think there are any links between what made you want to commit crimes before and what makes you want to write plays now?

When people end up in prison, they quite often discover an artistic side to themselves. But it's hard to keep hold of this once you've left prison, and a lot of people go back to crime again when they get out. Like in *Drummers* when Ray is looking at the house with the oak tree in Surrey and he says "Ah wanna paint its portrait not burgle the cunt, but ah can't fuckin' paint so..." . I suppose that writing or watching a play and going out to the country thieving are both kind of escapist. When you're writing a play you can control the outcome of events and dictate who gets caught and who gets away with it. Also, hopefully, you can create drama and excitement.

So when you went out thieving (drumming), were you motivated by something other than the money?

The money was important because it got you respect, good earners were respected. But when you're a thief you don't really value the money itself because you haven't earned it honestly - you just throw it away on things like drugs. That's why so many thieves become drug addicts. Drumming, especially when we went to the countryside, was also about getting away from the squalor of the town and finding a buzz. We were looking for adventure.

Is crime a subject that you want to continue exploring in your writing?

At the moment I'm drawing on my most recent experiences, but I definitely don't want my identity as a writer to be overshadowed by my past. Anyway, Drummers isn't really about crime. It's about love. It's about how love's not smooth. Especially in families. The characters just happen to be criminals.

Drummers isn't really about crime... It's about how love's not smooth. Especially in families.

Out of Joint was founded in 1993 by Max Stafford-Clark and Sonia Friedman to generate new writing for the stage and to tour this work nationally and internationally. Out of Joint consistently champions the work of contemporary writers, whether they are established figures such as Caryl Churchill or newcomers like Mark Ravenhill, whose first play, *Shopping and Fucking*, was such a remarkable success. In just over five years Out of Joint has produced a formidable body of work and has become a powerful new voice in British theatre. The company is increasingly in demand worldwide and much of its work remains in the repertoire for up to two years to enable further touring.

The plays produced have been enormously varied in style and matter. From Sue Townsend's satire about the Royal Family's exile to a Leicester council estate, *The Queen and I*, to Sebastian Barry's poetic drama *The Steward of Christendom*; and from the comedy and social realism of April de Angelis' *The Positive Hour*, to Caryl Churchill's inventive *Blue Heart*, the productions demonstrate the diversity that is Out of Joint's identity.

In 1997, Out of Joint's work was rewarded by a permanent commitment from the Arts Council of England. In its short life, Out of Joint has also received 17 major awards, including the Prudential Award for Theatre, and has been nominated for a further 16.

To date, Out of Joint has played in over 44 venues nationally and in a further 35 theatres worldwide.

"BRITAIN'S MOST SUCCESSFUL TOURING COMPANY"

THE STAGE

> *"The company has made a lasting impact on new writing in this country ... a quick glance at this year's activities alone gives you some impression of the extraordinary scale of Out of Joint's work"*
> The Independent

To stay fully informed, join Out of Joint's mailing list by sending your name, address and postcode (no stamp required within UK) to:

Mailing List, Out of Joint,
FREEPOST LON11065, LONDON N7 8BR
or contact: tel 0171 609 0207
fax 0171 609 0203
email: ojo@outofjoint.demon.co.uk

Out of Joint is grateful to the following for their support over the past five years:

The Foundation for Sport and the Arts, The Baring Foundation, The Paul Hamlyn Foundation, The Olivier Foundation, The Peggy Ramsay Foundation, The John S Cohen Foundation, The David Cohen Charitable Trust, the National Lottery through the Arts Council of England, The Prudential Awards, Stephen Evans, Karl Sydow.

Out of Joint international projects are supported by The British Council

Out of Joint's Productions

1994

Out of Joint's inaugural production paired a revival of **Road**, Jim Cartwright's mid-80's classic, with Sue Townsend's adaptation of her own hilarious novel, **The Queen and I**. The plays toured to packed houses and *The Queen and I* played for twelve weeks at the Royal Court Theatre before it transferred to the West End.

The company's second tour yoked **The Libertine**, Stephen Jeffreys' new biographical play about the Earl of Rochester, with a revival of his friend George Etherege's ground-breaking Restoration comedy **The Man of Mode**.

1995

Timberlake Wertenbaker wrote **The Break of Day** specifically to accompany Chekhov's **Three Sisters** and the two productions played at the Royal Court and on tour with the same company of actors. Out of Joint toured India with *Three Sisters* which also played a memorable season at Rossway Park, a large country house outside London.

The Steward of Christendom won much praise for writer Sebastian Barry, actor Donal McCann and director Max Stafford-Clark. It ran for two seasons at both the Royal Court Theatre and The Gate Theatre in Dublin and toured internationally including a highly successful season at BAM in New York.

1996

Mark Ravenhill's **Shopping and Fucking** began life at the tiny Royal Court Theatre Upstairs where it was hailed as a serious and remarkable debut. It has since completed sell-out runs at the Royal Court and in the West End as well as touring nationally and internationally.

Nigel Terry and Catherine Russell in *Three Sisters*

Donal McCann in *The Steward of Christendom*

Pearce Quigley and Caroline Catz in *Shopping and Fucking*

Photos: John Haynes

1997

Out of Joint co-produced April de Angelis' witty and astute social comedy **The Positive Hour** with Hampstead Theatre and toured it to Leeds, Cambridge, Liverpool, Watford, Warwick and Newcastle. Caryl Churchill's **Blue Heart**, marked the company's ninth co-production with the Royal Court Theatre. The play won a coveted Fringe First Award at the Edinburgh Festival before playing in London, across the country and in Egypt.

1998

In Out of Joint's busiest year to date, the company toured *Blue Heart* internationally whilst *Shopping and Fucking* undertook a further UK tour. Out of Joint commissioned Sebastian Barry to write **Our Lady of Sligo** for the company and this poetic memory play about the life of Mai O'Hara (Sinéad Cusack) played to full houses at the Royal National Theatre, at the Gate Theatre Dublin and on tour. Max Stafford-Clark's revival of **Our Country's Good** by Timberlake Wertenbaker was co-produced with the Young Vic Theatre and was enthusiastically received by critics and a very appreciative young audience.

1999

After *Blue Heart*'s New York premiere, Out of Joint embarked on a further tour of *Our Country's Good,* taking the company from Cambridge to Brazil, Israel, Bulgaria and Lithuania. In addition to Simon Bennett's **Drummers**, Out of Joint is also presenting the world premiere of **Some Explicit Polaroids,** an acerbic new satire from Mark Ravenhill.

For updated information on our future plans, join our mailing list.

David Sibley and Patti Love
in *The Positive Hour*

Valerie Lilley and Mary Macleod
in *Blue Heart*

Sinéad Cusack
in *Our Lady of Sligo*

Photos: John Haynes

OUT OF JOINT EDUCATION

Out of Joint is committed to providing educational work to complement its productions. Max Stafford-Clark has led over a hundred workshops and seminars for the Company, with positive feedback from students and teachers alike:

"Max Stafford-Clark was really great. I was wrong that he'd be a rich, upper-class, posh talking man who'd make me feel extremely intimidated. He appeared very down to earth and very dedicated to directing. He was very helpful and made us feel very comfortable."

"At the beginning of the workshop I felt very nervous...but I became more confident due to the activities. I would definitely like to do it again"

"Enormous value - we were able to see inside the world of the director from a professional and creative point of view...the level of work was demanding which was excellent"

"First class: I cannot imagine how the workshop could have been improved"

"Thank you so much for an inspiring day.. The students were thrilled to have taken part in the workshop and were awe-struck by the power of the production"

DRUMMERS EDUCATION PROGRAMME

Out of Joint is offering a full programme of education work to accompany the production, including workshops, free post-show discussions and a teachers' workpack.
For more information please contact Out of Joint on 0171 609 0207.

CO-PRODUCERS

Drummers is co-produced with Karl Sydow, Ambassador Theatre Group, Cambridge Arts Theatre and the Mercury Theatre, Colchester

KARL SYDOW

Formerly Chief Executive of First Call plc. Has produced / co-produced: *Macbeth, A Swell Party, Our Country's Good* (which was nominated for six Tony Awards and received the New York Critics' Award for Best Foreign Play), *Hysteria* (Best Comedy, Olivier Awards), *The Queen and I.* Karl is a Board member of Out of Joint.

AMBASSADOR THEATRE GROUP

Ambassador Theatre Group Ltd (ATG) has three main areas of activity: the ownership and management of theatre buildings, theatre production (in the West End but also nationally and internationally) and the development of new productions. ATG currently owns and operates the following arts buildings: The Duke of Yorks and the New Ambassadors in London, The New Victoria Theatre and Ambassadors Cinemas in Woking, The Victoria Hall and Regent Theatre in Stoke-on-Trent, The Milton Keynes Theatre and the historic Theatre Royal Brighton. It is also in the process of developing and acquiring other regional and London theatres.

ATG and its management company the Turnstyle Group Ltd, have a considerable track record in producing and co-producing for the West End and on national and international tours. Recent productions include: *Carmen Jones, The Rocky Horror Show, Smokey Joe's Cafe, The Royal Court Classics Season, Slava's Snow Show, The Late Middle Classes* and the Royal Court's Olivier Award winning play *The Weir* in London and on Broadway. They are about to produce a major new production of the classic musical *The Pajama Game* directed by Simon Callow.

In 1998 Sonia Friedman joined ATG as Producer where she is responsible for initiating, developing and producing a wide range of work for theatre across the West End, UK and internationally. From 1989 - 1993, Sonia was head of Mobile Productions and Theatre for Young People at the RNT where she was responsible for producing over 30 productions and projects. In 1993 Sonia co-founded Out of Joint with Max Stafford-Clark and has co-produced many productions with the Royal Court, RNT and Hampstead. In 1994 Sonia also produced *Maria Friedman by Special Arrangement* at the Donmar Warehouse.

AMBASSADORS THEATRE GROUP BOARD

Chairman	Sir Eddie Kulukundis OBE
Deputy Chairman	Peter Beckwith
Managing Director	Howard Panter
Executive Director	Rosemary Squire
Directors	David Beresford Jones, Miles Wilkin

FOR NEW AMBASSADORS THEATRE

Producer	Sonia Friedman	*Deputy LX*	Michelle Green
Head of Operations	David Blyth	*Master Carpenter*	Ivan Smith
Theatre Administrator	Tim Brunsden	*Deputy Carpenter*	Kevin Hough
Marketing	Jacqui Gellman	*Personnel Officer*	Maxi Harvey
	Lisa Popham	*Finance Consultant*	Judy Burridge
	for Dewynters	*Personnel Administrator*	Debbie Hill
Production Assistant	Amanda Murray	*Accountant*	Caroline Abrahams
Trainee Producer	Wade Kamaria	*Maintenance Technician*	Martin Hammond
Acting Deputy Manager	Rachel Fisher	*Stage Door Keeper*	Ben Till
Chief LX	Matthew O'Connor	*Relief Stage Door Keeper*	Sam Becker

Cambridge Arts Theatre

Cambridge Arts Theatre was founded in 1936 by the economist, John Maynard Keynes. It has been the launchpad for talents such as Trevor Nunn, Emma Thompson, Germaine Greer and John Cleese, and remains one of the most famous and well-loved venues in the country. With a varied programme of drama, dance, opera, music and comedy, and through an active education and community programme, the Theatre aims to develop high quality live performance which is enriching, enjoyable and accessible.

General Manager	Ian Ross
Head of Operations	Raymond Cross
Box Office Manager	Vivien Mayne
Front of House Manager	Rebecca Tullett
Finance Manager	Lisa Winter
Marketing Manager	Nicola Upson
Education Manager	Roberta Hamond

The Mercury Theatre, opened in 1972, presents a mixed programme of its own productions, visiting and co-produced work in both the main house and the Mercury Studio. The theatre also provides an extensive range of youth and community activities.

The last year has seen the establishment of a resident company of actors at the theatre. The first season performed by the Mercury Theatre Company this spring included an acclaimed production of Chekhov's *Uncle Vanya* and the British premiere of *Don Juan on Trial* by Eric-Emmanuel Schmitt.

"The Mercury's new chief Executive Dee Evans is lining up an ambitious programme with a resident company, and she has strong support from Colchester Borough Council, which wants the town to have a producing theatre. Other councils please take note"
SUNDAY TIMES

DRUMMERS

BY SIMON BENNETT

Cast in alphabetical order:

Barry
Callum Dixon

George
Ewan Hooper

Ella
Maggie McCarthy

Pete
Paul Ritter

Ray
Peter Sullivan

Director
Max Stafford-Clark

Designer
Nathalie Gibbs

Lighting Designer
Johanna Town

Sound Designer
John Harris

Assistant Directors
Gillian King, Joe White

Casting Director
Lisa Makin

Fight Director
Terry King

Production Management
Phil Cameron, Richard Blacksell
for Background Production Limited

Company and Stage Manager
Sylvia Carter

Deputy Stage Manager
Sally McKenna

Assistant Stage Manager
Ian Shillito

Production Electrician
Tim Bray

Costume Supervisor
Charlotte Stewart

Wardrobe Mistress
Lesley Huckstepp

Production Photography
John Haynes

Rehearsal Photography
Charlie Crane

For Out of Joint:

Producer
Graham Cowley

Marketing Manager
Madeline Joinson

Press
Cameron Duncan PR

Administrator
Suzannah Bedford

Admin and Marketing Assistant
Alice Lascelles

Production credits: Set built by Mercury Theatre Workshops; Jewellery by Jenny Ogunsiji. **With special thanks to** Kings Cross Snooker Club

SIMON BENNETT (writer)

Simon was born in 1967 and grew up in Brixton Hill where the action for Drummers is set. At the age of twenty, Simon began a two year sentence for burglary at HMP Winchester and it was during this time that he began writing. Following his release in 1989, Simon attended a Theatre Studies course at Merton College in the evenings whilst working as a painter and decorator during the day. He wrote the first draft of Drummers during this period. The play was subsequently workshopped at the Royal Court's Youth Theatre in 1992. Tattooed Tears, another early play, was also workshopped at the Royal Court Theatre by Ian Rickson and was later a finalist in the Allied Domecq New Playwrights Competition at the Bush Theatre.

CALLUM DIXON (Barry)

Callum recently appeared as Harry in *A Real Classy Affair* at the Royal Court Theatre. Other theatre credits include Lee Finch in *Faith* and Sweets in *Mojo* for the Royal Court Theatre, Nat in *Deadwood* at the Watermill Theatre, and seasons at the Royal Shakespeare Company. For the Royal National Theatre he has played Horace in *The Day I Stood Still*, Alfred in *Rosencrantz and Guildenstern are Dead*, Norman in *The Wind in the Willows* and Thomas in *The Recruiting Officer*. He also played Cambell in *Somewhere* for a Royal National Theatre Studio tour. Other work includes *The Bill*, *The Queen's Nose* and *Hetty Wainthropp Investigates*, all for television, *The Wolfgang Chase* for BBC Radio and the film *Waterlands*.

NATHALIE GIBBS (Designer)

Nathalie trained at St Martin's School of Art and Design and Motley Theatre Design Course. She has worked on a numerous productions including *Dogs Barking* (Bush Theatre); Peter Gill's *Certain Young Men* (Almeida); *Macbeth* (English Touring Opera); *The Overcoat* (The Clod Ensemble); and Fraser Trainer's *The Knack* (English National Opera Contemporary Opera Studios). As well as working in film and as a scenic painter for the Royal National Theatre, she has also assisted on productions at the Royal Court Theatre, Glyndebourne and abroad. Forthcoming projects include; *A Midsummer Night's Dream* (National Youth Theatre); *Hyacinth Blue* (Clean Break); costume deisgn for *Triumph of Love* (Almeida).

JOHN HARRIS (Sound Designer)

John's frequent projects at the Traverse, Edinburgh include *Family; Perfect Days* (also on tour in Scotland); *Anna Weiss; Knives in Hens; Greta* and *Sharp Shorts*. Other theatre work includes: *Stockaree; Of Nettles and Roses* (Theatre Workshop); *Not for the Fanfare* (First Base); *The Nest; M'Lady Malade; The Great Theatre of the World; Mankind; The Tempest* (True Belleek). Musical direction includes: *Mass* by Leonard Bernstein and *Carmina Burana* by Carl Orff. John is also commissioned as a classical composer, and recent work has included the composition of fanfares for the Kirking of the Scottish Parliament. He also works as Assistant Organist at St Giles' Cathedral, Edinburgh, broadcasting and recording regularly.

EWAN HOOPER (George)

Recent theatre includes: Out of Joint's production of *Blue Heart; King Lear* (Young Vic, Japanese tour); *Hindle Wakes* (Royal

Exchange); *The Woman in Black* (Fortune Theatre); *Toast* (Royal Court Theatre). Other theatre credits include: *The Broken Heart; Coriolanus; Henry V: The Caretaker* (Royal Shakespeare Company); *The Changing Room; The Kitchen; Hammet's Apprentice; All Things Nice; Falkland Sound/Gibraltar Strait; Bingo* (Royal Court Theatre); *Richard II; The Recruiting Officer; The Doctor's Dilemma; She Stoops to Conquer; Much Ado About Nothing* (Royal Exchange); *The Tempest* (Bristol Old Vic); *A Hard Heart* (Almeida); *Roots* (Royal National Theatre). Television includes *Roots; Across the Lake; Irons of Wrath; Hi de Hi; King Lear; Invasion* and the long running series *Hunter's Walk*. Film credits include *Personal Services; Julius Caesar; How I Won the War; Dracula Has Risen from the Grave.*

GILLIAN KING (Assistant Director)

As an Assistant Director, Gillian has worked at the Northcott Theatre, Exeter on *Twelfth Night* and *Richard IV* and co-directed *Far From The Madding Crowd*. She has also worked at the King's Head Theatre and subsequently toured as staff director on the King's Head/Churchill Theatre Bromley No. 1 tour of *Cavalcade*. Other Assistant credits include *The Return of Martin Guerre* (VF Productions); *Joined at the Head* (WTW small-scale tour) and *Richard III* (Original Shakespeare Company). Her previous directing credits include *The Illusion; A Family Affair; The Suicide* and *Frankenstein* (all London fringe); *Macbeth* and *Romeo and Juliet* for school tours. Most recently Gillian was Education Director for *Hamlet* at Greenwich Theatre, and directed *Belgrade Trilogy* for the Tricycle Theatre.

MAGGIE MCCARTHY (Ella)

Theatre Maggie's extensive theatre credits include: *The Steward of Christendom* (Out of Joint/Royal Court); Fekushla in *The Storm* (Almeida); *Thickness of Skin; The Seagull; Byrthrite* (Royal Court); *Mountain Giants; Macbeth; Night of the Iguana; The Shaughraun; Fanshen* (Royal National Theatre); *Sailor Beware* (Lyric Hammersmith); *Cat With Green Violin* (Orange Tree); *Golden Pathway Annual* (Mayfair); *The Crucible* (Young Vic); *The Garden Girls* (Bush Theatre). She also has numerous television credits including *Berkeley Square; Hello Girls; All Quiet on the Preston Front; Casualty; Tumbledown; Softly Softly* (BBC); *She's Out* (Cinema Verity). Films include *Firelight; Hilary and Jackie,* and the soon to be released *Angela's Ashes* and *Esther Khan.*

PAUL RITTER (Pete)

Theatre includes *Three Sisters* (Oxford Stage Company tour & West End); *Bluebird* (Royal Court Theatre Upstairs); *Belle Fontaine* (Soho Theatre Company); *Grab the Dog* (Royal National Theatre Studio); *Happy Valley* (Liverpool Everyman). At the Bush Theatre: *Crossing the Equator; Raising Fires; Darwin's Flood.* At the Gate Theatre: *A Little Satire; Time & The Room; The Great Highway.* For the Royal Shakespeare Company: *Troilus and Cressida; The White Devil; Three Hours After Marriage.* Film and television includes: *Esther Kahn* (Zenith Films); *The Nine Lives of Tomas Katz (Strawberry Vale Film and TV); The Bill* (Thames); *National Achievement Day* (BBC2); *Big Cat* (BBC1); *Out of Hours* (BBC1) and *GMT* (Anvil Films). For Radio 4: *Thrush Green; Agent 52; Grease Monkeys* and *Skin Deep.*

MAX STAFFORD-CLARK (Director)

Educated at Trinity College, Dublin. Founded Joint Stock Theatre group in 1974 following his Artistic Directorship of The Traverse Theatre, Edinburgh. From 1979 to 1993 he was Artistic Director of The Royal Court Theatre. In 1993 he founded Out of Joint. His work as a Director has overwhelmingly been with new writing, and he has commissioned and directed first productions by many of the country's leading writers.

PETER SULLIVAN (Ray)

A graduate of Central School of Speech and Drama, Peter has worked extensively in theatre, film and television, both in the UK and abroad. Recent theatre productions include *Certain Young Men* (Almeida) and *Night of the Assassins* (Lyric Hammersmith). He is a member of the Spanish performance group La Fura Dels Baus. Peter has also appeared in several Royal National Theatre productions including Richard Eyre's *Richard III* and *King Lear* directed by Deborah Warner. Television work includes the series *Backup; Over the Rainbow; Hope and Glory* and *Heat of the Sun.*

JOHANNA TOWN (Lighting Designer)

Johanna has been Head of Lighting for the Royal Court Theatre since 1990 and has designed extensively for the company during this time. Productions include: *The Kitchen, Faith Healer, Pale Horse, Search and Destroy, Women Laughing, Neverland.* Theatre credits over the past year include: *Rose* (Royal National Theatre); *Little Malcolm and His Struggle Against the Eunuchs* (Hampstead & West End), *Our Country's Good,* (Out of Joint/Young Vic), *Our Lady of Sligo* (Out of Joint/Royal National Theatre); *Blue Heart* (Out of Joint, New York); *Choice* and *Toast* (Royal Court Upstairs). Opera credits include *Tobias and The Angel* (Almeida Opera Factory); *La Boheme* and *Die Fledermaus* (MTL). Johanna is currently working on the refurbishment of the Royal Court in Sloane Square.

JOE WHITE (Assistant Director)

Most recently, Joe assisted on Out of Joint's production of *Our Country's Good.* During his thirteen years of imprisonment he was involved in the production and promotion of theatre as both director and performer. Prison productions include: *East; The Love of a Good Man; Our Country's Good; Crime and Punishment; Death and the Maiden* and *The Possibilities.* He has assisted Steven Pimlott's *Vieux Carre* (Nottingham Playhouse) and Nicholas de Jongh's *Traveller Without Luggage* (BAC). He has also contributed a chapter 'The Prisoner's Voice' to the publication *Prison Theatre: Perspectives and Practices.*

To Grandad

DRUMMERS

Simon Bennett

To Grandad

Characters

PETE, *late thirties, son of George*

GEORGE, *early sixties*

RAY, *early thirties*

BARRY, *late twenties, brother of Ray*

ELLA, *early fifties, mother of Ray and Barry*

Most of the action takes place in the back room of a small pool hall, situated on the back streets of South London.

There are two exits. The left exit leads to the pool tables and the front entrance. The right exit leads to the toilet and another exit that leads on to the street.

A round table sits in front of the left exit, surrounded by well worn armchairs of different descriptions. An old grey till sits on top of a table, in front of the right exit. A cupboard is fixed to the wall above the till.

ACT ONE

Scene One

Three men sit at the table. PETE *holds a thick gold chain in the air, studying it through a magnifying glass.* RAY *rolls a spliff.* BARRY *sits the other side of* PETE *watching him.*

PETE. Yer right Ray, it's twenny-two.

RAY. An 'ah don' need a lookin' glass either.

PETE. Well ah know from experience that colour don' dictate the carat.

PETE *drops the chain on the table.* RAY *picks it up.*

RAY. Ah don' see twenny-two, ah feel it.

PETE. Alright Uri, stick it in the twenny-two bag.

PETE *throws a small money bag across the table at* RAY.

RAY. Ah ain' sellin' this for scrap, when ah can get two an' alf in Brixton for it.

PETE. Tha's if the cunts don' rob ya first.

BARRY. Jus' get rid of it now Ray.

RAY. Ya get one fifty scrap if ya lucky. Wait one night an' 'ah'll get us another oner.

BARRY. Ya carn trus' them bods down there. Fulla fuckin' crack 'eads.

PETE. Steal the air ya breathe, if it sold. I know mate.

RAY. Barry mentioned ya was robbed, wot 'appened?

PETE. Three bods, robbed the place.

RAY. So ya reckon they're Brixton bods?

PETE. No one on this manna's gonna rob me. An I tell ya wot, them cunts won' be comin' back in a 'urry. No sooner 'ad the firs' one got through the door 'e was sprawled out on the deck.

RAY. Wot, 'e jus' threw 'imself on the floor?

PETE. No I fuckin' 'it the cunt. The second one I 'ad across the table about ta knock the shit out of 'im, when a third one pops up from nowhere an' sticks a tool to me throat. An' I don' give fuck who you are, when ya feel that cold blade touch ya adam's apple . . . All I 'ad was a score an' a couple o' rings. Ain' gonna die for that. But I tell ya wot mate, they could fuckin' move, cos no sooner 'as that blade left me throat, I 'ad the chair in me 'ands, jus' caught the las' one on the shoulder, 'urt 'im cos 'e fuckin' squealed. Any'ow where I've lobbed the chair at 'em it's blocked the fuckin' doorway an' I've gone arse over tit tryin' ta get at the cunts, en I. Felt a right mug. But I tell ya, they come again.

PETE *suddenly goes under the table, he is heard tugging at something and after a few moments, he stands holding a knife. Bits of tape hang from the blade.*

RAY *and* BARRY *stare at him.* RAY *is unimpressed, he takes a puff on his spliff and blows a smoke ring towards* PETE. *He picks up the chain and puts it in his pocket.* PETE *throws the knife down on the table.*

PETE. Don' say we didn' warn ya.

RAY *looks at some rings on the table.*

RAY. What we lookin' for, items?

PETE. Two.

RAY. There's more than two there.

PETE. I'll give ya two for now an' when I offload 'em I'll give ya the rest.

PETE *goes to the till, opens it and brings out a set of electric scales.* RAY *stares at* BARRY *as he lights a spliff.* BARRY *looks back at him.*

BARRY. Wot the fuck's wrong wi' you?

RAY *shrugs.*

RAY. Doctors with degrees couldn' work it out. Wot fuckin' chance 'ave ah got?

PETE *puts the scales on the table. He picks up a money bag of gold and throws it on.*

PETE. Tha's ya nine, 'undred an' twenny-three.

RAY *leans over and looks at the scales.* PETE *jots the number down on a note pad.* PETE *replaces the money bag with another.*

PETE. Seventy-eight ya eighteen.

RAY *leans over again and checks the scales.* PETE *jots it down.*

PETE. And lastly, ya twenny-two.

PETE *throws on the money bag.* RAY *looks at the scales.* PETE *jots it down.* PETE *starts doing sums on a piece of paper. He holds up the completed sum for* RAY *and* BARRY *to read. They both nod.* PETE *takes a thick roll of money from his pocket, starts counting it on the table.*

BARRY. Well tha's a lot better than las' time.

RAY. Fuckin' shit.

BARRY. Never satisfied are ya?

PETE *finishes counting,* RAY *picks up the money and starts counting* BARRY*'s share out on to the table in front of him.*

RAY. Plus ya got one twenny ta come for the chain.

PETE *starts putting away the scales and gold. He goes to the till and puts the gold inside. He returns to the table as* RAY *and* BARRY *put their money away. He holds up a ring.*

PETE. Wot would ya take fo' this?

RAY *takes the ring.*

PETE. Remember it's me ya takin' from.

RAY. A couple o' gran' in that case.

PETE. Be serious.

RAY. Fifty.

> RAY *passes the ring to* BARRY, *who shrugs and gives it back to* PETE.

PETE. Ya get twenny scrap at the most.

RAY. Ah'm not sellin' it fo' scrap.

PETE. Fuck ya then.

RAY. Oh go on then Petey.

PETE. Fifteen?

RAY. Nah Fifty.

> PETE *puts the ring in his pocket.*

BARRY. A present for the misses?

PETE. Nah, Maureen. Jus' a little thank you fo' the other night.

BARRY. 'ow did the big night go then?

PETE. Nice of you ta ask, two fuckin' days later.

BARRY. Ah'm askin' now.

RAY. Ain'adda night out in years.

BARRY. 'e took Maureen to a show.

PETE. 'adda meal first.

RAY. Lovely.

PETE. Took 'er to a gaff uptown, well posh, a jacks for two coffees, should give ya sum idea of wot ah'm talkin' about. The meal alone came ta forty quid.

RAY. Did ya feel out o' place?

PETE. Not at all. Granted they all 'ad plums in their mouths but you shouldda seen the tom. There was this one ol' bird, must 'ad an 'undred thousan' roun' er neck alone. Ah thought about callin' a couple o' bods down ta 'it 'er on the way out, but ah 'ad more important things doing.

RAY (*to* BARRY). Tha's why we don' go out nights an' weekends.

BARRY. A'right Ray, I got the message.

RAY. Took ya fuckin' time about it..

PETE. Ah right pair o' tarts, you two.

BARRY. Wot show did ya go an' see, Pete?

PETE. Ah took 'er to see the Buddy Holly Story.

BARRY. She enjoy it?

PETE. Loved it, 'ad the time of 'er fuckin' life. She told me after, that it was the bes' night out she's ever 'ad. Ah paid for the meal with that book an' card Terry Bell sold me.

BARRY. The Rupert Hume one.

PETE. Ah thought payin' in cash was a bit common. So ah got out me gold pen an' wrote a cheque. Got the signiture off to a tee.

BARRY. Don' get me wrong Pete, but you don' look like a Rupert.

PETE. Listen mate, you get suited an' booted, 'an a bit o' tom roun' ya neck, put on a posh accent, you can get away with murder. Cunts didn' look twice, gave me the receipt, thanked me for me custom, very polite they were, callin' me sir an'er madam. We took a taxi to the show. Shouldda seen 'er, balled 'er fuckin' eyes out at the end.

BARRY. Why's that then?

PETE. 'e dies, dunn'e.

BARRY. Who does?

PETE. Buddy 'olly ya cunt. Died in a plane crash.

BARRY. Oh right.

PETE. Well tha's why she cried. Mus' admit ah felt a bit choked at the end.

BARRY. 'ow did they get a plane on to the stage?

RAY *starts laughing. Relights his spliff.*

RAY. Mum likes Buddy 'olly, or used to.

BARRY. Still does.

PETE. Ah think 'e's a top bod, fuck Elvis.

BARRY. She likes 'im better.

RAY. Only when 'e sung that gosbal shit.

PETE. Then ah brought 'er back 'ere.

RAY *and* BARRY *wait for him to continue.*

PETE. Well ah think you know the rest. Without goin' inta too
    much detail, we wen' at it like a pair o' love sick 'urricanes.
    The chair ya sittin' on Bal, wuz brought into the picture, not
    ta mention the pool tables. Ah did finally manage ta get 'er
    in the sack.

BARRY *stands and looks at the seat.*

RAY. Two quid for a coffee, musta bin posh.

PETE. Propah upperclass gaff, pure socialites.

BARRY. Wossa solialite?

RAY. Someone who pays fo' meals wi' their own cheque book.

PETE. Ah chose not ta pay fo' the meal.

RAY. Cameras everywhere these days.

BARRY. Tha's true.

PETE. They wouldda chored me by now.

RAY. The cheque wouldn'ave cleared yet. You gotta watch
    yaself these days.

PETE. Naa bollox, they ain' gettin' me. Not this one mate.

RAY. Maureen . . . That was that fat spotty cunt used ta 'ang
    roun' with the black salt.

BARRY *laughs.*

PETE. She ain' fat, she's got no spots an' she don' 'ang roun' wi' the black salt anymore. She can be a bit of a cunt sometimes so I'll give ya that one.

RAY. Wot was 'er name . . . ?

PETE. Dawn.

RAY. Tha's it. Now that wazza salt.

PETE. She was alright, wouldn' fuck a black bird meself. 'ad plenny o' chances, but ya know . . . I'm not a racialist or anything, jus'ain' into 'em, tha's all.

RAY. Ah bet she's at college now.

PETE. Training to be a socialite. Proper little madam that one. Never smoked, drank or swore. Sung Halleluyah in church every Sunday . . . Eighteen an' bet she ain' even 'adda fuck yet.

RAY. She could afford to be choosey.

BARRY. Ah must admit. Ya got a lovely wife an' ya risk it all for a shag.

PETE. Ah know 'ow lovely me wife is.

BARRY. Ar'm jus' sayin . . . Ah mean Ray's right, Maureen is a right pig ent she?

PETE. You tried shaggin' it long before me, cunt.

BARRY. Got the wrong bod.

PETE. Johnnie Mace's party, said you was on 'er case all night.

BARRY. Ah was pissed out me nut that night, if sum cunt put a skirt on the dog ah'd a tried an' got a shag out of it. An' that was a scabby little mongral as well.

PETE. As well as wot?

BARRY. Well . . .

RAY. Maureen.

PETE. Ya jus' jealous cos you ain' adda fuck in years.

RAY. Show us ya posh accent Pete.

PETE. Yer wot?

RAY. You said if ya get suited an' booted, with a posh accent, you can get away with murder.

BARRY. Yeh, go on Pete.

PETE. Alright, a'right . . . Excus . . . 'old on . . . Excuse me sir, could ah have a bottle of ya finest wine . . .

Silence. RAY *and* BARRY *look at each other.*

RAY. Don' ever murder anyone will ya Pete?

PETE. Na, ah got bods that do that sort o' thing for me.

RAY. Shouldda got um ta sign the kite.

PETE. Ah'm sweet mate, don' worry bout me.

RAY. Standin' in the dock, fo' fraud, over one poxy meal, won' do ya rep any good.

PETE. Ar've paid fo' a 'undred meals with a 'undred dodgy books an' me reps still intact. So the pair of ya can shut ya mouth an' yes the meal was lovely. Ah thought me an' my brother were bad.

RAY. 'ow is 'enry these days, still knockin' out dodgy motors?

PETE. A millionaire, 'ow would you be?

RAY. Stoned.

PETE. Ya don' need a million to be stoned. You of all people should know that.

RAY. Ar'm talkin' about proper stoned, not this shit. I tell ya when they process the stuff, abroad, yer know the shit at the bottom of the barrel? They lump it together an' stamp it England, them cunts'll smoke anything. Even the browns cut ta fuck before it reaches 'ere.

PETE. Not my brown pal.

RAY. Wot about yours Bal?

BARRY. What is it that makes you think that I'm on the gear?

RAY. Mus' be that dead look in ya eyes.

BARRY. Ya the dead one.

PETE. So you're sayin' you'd leave the country for a decent puff?

RAY. Before you could say, two ounces please sir. But not in that posh accent of yours ey.

PETE. Well le's face it Ray, you ain' never gonna be a millionaire.

RAY. Not with the way things are goin', ey Bal?

BARRY. An' tha's my fault?

PETE. Oy don' start all that again. It's a bad patch, soon it'll be over.

RAY stands and lights his spliff again.

PETE. Maureen ain' that bad is she?

Silence.

RAY (*to* BARRY). She still got all that wire mesh roun' er teeth?

BARRY. She should 'ave, an' a magnet under 'er chin ta keep 'er mouth shut.

PETE takes out the ring and throws it on the table.

PETE. Keep ya fuckin' ring.

BARRY picks up the ring and hands it to PETE.

BARRY. We're only fuckin' about Pete.

RAY. Barry, ya ready?

BARRY. You don' wanna lift 'ome do ya?

RAY. Ah didn' put 'alf the money towards that car ta walk everywhere, did I?

BARRY. Ar'm gonna play me music.

RAY. Tha's nice for ya.

BARRY. You'll soon start complainin'.

RAY. The fact that you play such shit isn't the source of my complaint. What do bods do when ah car goes past um blarin' soun's?

BARRY. Who gives a fuck.

RAY. Me, cos they look. An' do we want bods lookin' at the car when we're graftin'? No. Play ya shit as loud as ya like.

RAY *throws his spliff in the ashtray.*

RAY. See ya later Pete.

RAY *exits.* BARRY *waits until he has gone.*

BARRY. I'll be back in a while.

PETE. A'right mate.

BARRY *exits.*

Blackout.

Scene Two

PETE *sits at the table. We hear the sound of someone letting themselves in.* PETE *quickly gathers up a plastic bag of works: spoon, needle etc that's lying on the table. He runs to the cupboard, climbs on a chair beneath it and throws the bag on top.* GEORGE *enters through the right exit.*

PETE. Alright, Dad?

GEORGE. Sweet as.

PETE *sits back at the table.* GEORGE *lays his paper down on the table. Takes out a cigarette, lights it and sits down. He opens his paper and begins reading.*

PETE. Ah think ah'll 'ave a little flutter today.

GEORGE. Oh yeh.

PETE. Ah got a couple of tips . . .

Silence. GEORGE *continues reading his paper.*

PETE. Dad?

GEORGE. Wot?

PETE. Ah said ah got a couple of tips.

GEORGE. Well keep um to yaself a son.

PETE. 'enry give um ta me.

GEORGE. When did you see 'enry?

PETE. Couple o' days ago. As it goes 'e should be 'ere soon.

GEORGE. Ah doubt that.

PETE. 'e's gotta gimme some reddies, so you can doubt all ya want.

GEORGE. Unless the London ta Manchester does U turns ah shall doubt all ah want.

PETE. Ah don' believe it, I really fuckin' don't. No disrespect to 'enry, Dad, but 'e comes in 'ere with the rarin' 'ump sometimes. Gives me a right 'ard time about the state of the tables, the bog stinkin', cue tips missin'. No chalk. Questions whether I'm fit enough to run the gaff. Now 'e does this to me. An' 'e said to me 'e weren' pickin' the motors up till Thursday, I remember it clearly.

GEORGE. It is Thursday. ya mug.

PETE. Is it? Oh. Well, wot am I gonna tell me drummers?

GEORGE. Ya better go to the bank then, ent ya?

PETE. You love it don't ya?

GEORGE. Do ya want me ta give it to ya?

PETE. Don' take the piss, Dad.

GEORGE *pulls a wad of notes out of his pocket.*

GEORGE. 'ow much wuzzit?

PETE. You can stop, Dad, coz ah ain' fallin' for it.

GEORGE. Eight 'undred wunnit?

GEORGE starts counting the money.

PETE. Ah don't want ya money dad.

GEORGE. Four 'undred.

GEORGE continues counting.

GEORGE. Well would you fuckin' Adam an' Eve it? Eight 'undred exactly. Tha's wot ya wanted wunnit.

Pause.

PETE. Is that mine?

GEORGE. Ah don' even wunnit back.

PETE. You fuckin' wind up merchant.

PETE snatches the money from the table. GEORGE flicks his paper and continues reading. PETE recounts the money.

GEORGE. Woss this tip then?

Pause as PETE counts the money.

PETE. Can ya look after the shop fo' a while?

GEORGE. Tha's a long name for a 'orse.

PETE. Jolly Boy, three-thirty, Kempton.

GEORGE. Ah told 'enry about that one. Ya said ya 'ad a couple?

PETE. Sonny reckons Jakes Straw, Epsom.

GEORGE bursts out laughing.

GEORGE. 'e's a right barsted that geezah.

PETE. Ar've also done me 'omework on it.

GEORGE. Oh yeh?

PETE. See Dad, it's bin rainin' all night an' any cunt'll tell ya, that 'orse loves the wet ground.

GEORGE. Slide along on its arse does it?

PETE. A'right we'll see.

GEORGE. Fuckin' 'orse ain' fit ta carry kids up an' down Margate beach.

PETE. Are ya gonna look after the place or not?

GEORGE. 'Ow long ya gonna be?

PETE. Jus' gotta sell a bit o' tom.

GEORGE. Well if ya too long, ah'll close up an' piss off.

PETE *holds up the money.*

PETE. Three 'undred poun' fo' sittin' on me arse.

GEORGE. Ah'm proud of ya son.

PETE. Don' start dishin' out ya pride jus' yet.

GEORGE. You jus' tell when then son.

PETE. Ar've never made you proud 'ave I, Dad?

GEORGE. Not in recent times, no.

PETE. . . . If Barry comes in, give 'im this.

PETE *hands* GEORGE *some money.*

PETE. Tell 'im ah'll see 'im later . . .

GEORGE. Don' be long.

PETE *exits.* GEORGE *looks about the room. He stares at the cupboard fixed to the wall. He gets up, dragging the chair with him, he goes to the cupboard. He climbs up on the chair, opens the cupboard and looks inside.*

RAY *enters and watches as* GEORGE *stretches, trying to reach the top of the cupboard. Unable to, he gets down.*

RAY. Ya didn' see Barry up there did ya?

GEORGE. A'right Ray. Ah was jus' er, ya know. Ah los' something . . .

RAY. Right . . . No Barry then?

GEORGE. Well 'e ain' on top o' the cupboard . . . Ain'e at 'ome?

RAY. Probably.

RAY turns to leave.

GEORGE. 'old on Ray.

RAY stops.

GEORGE. Ah ain' seen ya fo' three years mate. Sit down for a minute.

RAY sits down. GEORGE pulls the chair back to the table and sits opposite RAY. He offers his hand across the table to RAY. RAY takes it.

GEORGE. It's good ta see ya mate.

RAY. Is it?

GEORGE. Yeh it is. So 'ow's it goin'?

RAY. It takes a while ta get into the swing of things.

GEORGE. I was startin' ta feel a bit offended, ah mean ya bin out a month an' ya ain' come ta see me.

RAY. I was plannin' to . . .

GEORGE. . . . . Shame about Joey ennit?

RAY. Yeh.

GEORGE. Musta bin a shock for ya.

RAY. Carnt really remember 'ow ah felt.

GEORGE. Ya got me letter then?

RAY. Yeh . . . Sorry ah didn' write back.

GEORGE. Ah thought it was only right you should know. You was good mates . . .

RAY. We was yeh.

GEORGE. Such a good drummer, which begs the question. 'ow the fuck did 'e fall out a window?

RAY. Probably off 'is 'ead on something or other. I always said the drugs would kill 'im in the end.

GEORGE. Wot 'appened between you an' 'im that day?

RAY. I'd 'ad enough, tha's wot 'appened. 'e's walkin' roun'
the drum not knowin' wot fuckin' day it is . . . 'e's sayin'
'e's searched but when ah search again, I'm findin' things.
A gold fuckin' egg, 'e went right past it.

GEORGE. Egg, as in Fabergé?

RAY. Imitation I reckon. Propah gold, eigh'een kay. Then the
cunt starts talkin' about trust . . . An' ah lost it a bit.

RAY *pulls a half smoked spliff from his pocket and lights it.*

GEORGE. What I carn understand is, if 'e gets away with all
the tom, 'ow comes you still copped a three for the drum?

RAY. Didn't ya speak ta Joey?

GEORGE. 'e was vague ta say the very fuckin' least. 'e said a
car pulled out in front of 'im.

RAY. 'e missed the car. I mean credit where it's due. Drivin'
into a ditch, sendin' me through the windscreen, knockin'
me clean out on the fuckin' bonnet, 'is credit suddenly
expired.

RAY *starts to roll another spliff.*

GEORGE. 'e didn' say that.

RAY. Ah bet 'e fuckin' never.

GEORGE. So 'ow d'ya get charged for the drum?

RAY. I come aroun' an' the car's surrounded by gavvers. An' as
they pulled me off, the egg rolled across the bonnet in full
view.

GEORGE. Tha's bollocks mate . . . Ya know if ya learnt ta
drive ya wouldn' need anyone.

RAY. 'ow many years ya bin tellin' me that?

GEORGE. Ya think ah'da givin' up by now. Woss ya bruvvah
like?

RAY. Not bad.

GEORGE. Ah was surprised ya went back out there. You get chored again ya lookin' at a five, yer know that don't ya?

RAY. Where else can ah go?

GEORGE. You could get a job.

Pause as RAY *takes in the last sentence.*

GEORGE. I'm sorry. Don' mind me, I'm old fashioned. Get a job, what was I thinkin'.

RAY. The ole man worked all 'is life, all 'e 'ad was the box they buried 'im in.

GEORGE. At least ya earnin'.

RAY. Yehh, who told ya that then?

GEORGE. Pete's flush at the moment.

RAY. Is 'e?

GEORGE. Owed 'enry two gran'. Paid the lot in the las' month . . . Tough one this time wunnit?

RAY. Wot the bird?

GEORGE. Tha's wot ah 'eard like.

RAY. Nahh, the cunts bang me up ah jus' jump in bed an' sleep it off. There were times in there, when ah didn' wanna be anywhere else . . . Barry is a good drummah . . .

GEORGE. Seen ya mum?

RAY. Nah. She don' wanna see me . . . I always thought Christianity was about forgiveness.

GEORGE. Don' jump to conclusions until you've seen 'er. I'm not sayin' it's gonna be roses, given ya past I doubt it will be, but don' go makin' up ya mind mate. I mean ya didn' burn the whole church down. It was open a few months later, it was in the local press.

RAY. Still gimme two an'alf in Rochester. I reckon the judge was a fuckin' Christian.

GEORGE. Two an'alf ain' bad fo' arson. Ya mum's jus' like a lot o' people, they fin' comfort in the Lord. An' tha's all it is Ray. Me ole man never wen' into a church in 'is whole life. But on 'is death bed would look to the ceilin' an beg forgiveness for 'is sins. 'e'd gone completely senile by then, but ya know, comfort.

RAY. Did ya ole man 'ave a lot of sins ta confess?

GEORGE. Dunno. I do know 'e worked like a dog in that timber yard an' died wi' a lung fulla sawdust.

RAY. Them sins are not for the likes of us to be confessing.

GEORGE. No one does nuffin' for ya in this life.

RAY. Nah, ya gotta take it yaself.

GEORGE. I always liked workin' wi' you. No bollocks. Do ya business, keep ya mouth shut, the way it should be . . . There were some good days back then. Joey an' the others could be pricks sometimes, but still. Gooddays.

RAY. They were gooddays.

GEORGE. Not so now. Pete should go into the waste disposal game, cos anything 'e touches, runs straight into the fuckin' ground an' disappears. 'e's me son bless 'im, but 'e's fuckin' useless. A few years ago I would 'ave foun' that 'ard to say, not now though. Ah used ta get a good wage outta them pool tables alone. Naa the fuckin' things don' even pay the rent. I think 'e's back on the heroin. You ain' seen anything 'ave ya?

RAY. Nah.

GEORGE. You wouldn' say anyway would ya? . . . Well if ya not earnin' wot 'e says you are. Then my guess is that 'e's sellin' it as well. 'e ain' doin' it from 'ome, I know that much. 'e must be knockin' it out from 'ere . . . I'm too fuckin' old for all this.

Pause. RAY *lights his spliff,* GEORGE *a cigarette.*

GEORGE. If Pete is back on it, then it's a strong possibility ya brother is too.

RAY. I'll soon find out if 'e is. Ah passed the cafe, looks nice.

GEORGE. Me pride an' joy that place. Did ya go in?

RAY. Na ah jus' passed.

GEORGE. 'ad it all done out las' year. Cos' nearly twenny gran'. Ah put in all new cookers, the works. An ah mus' say ah'm gettin' a better class o' punter in there. Money well spent that.

RAY. Ah noticed Brixton's gettin' a bit up-market these days.

GEORGE. Ya know ah'll always do ya a breakfas' Ray, I shouldn'ave ta tell ya that.

RAY. Ah'm graftin' tomorrow, wouldn' min' a breakfas' ta set me up for the day.

GEORGE. Well come in an' fill ya stomach. We'll 'ave a proper chat. The cafe's a good place ta do that, ya got the privacy of people.

RAY. It's gonna be a good day tomorrow. Before ah wen' inside ah was doggin' this drum for weeks. Ah'd forgot all about it. The other day we're on a scountin' mission, turn the corner an bosh! It's right there in front of me. Ah nearly made Barry crash the car.

RAY *rises.*

Fuckin' beautiful drum . . . It's jus' set back off the road a bit. This fuck off oak stands proud on the front lawn, unbelievable sight on a misty mornin'. Ah wanna paint its portrait not burgle the cunt, but ah can't fuckin' paint so . . .

GEORGE. What can ya do?

GEORGE *also rises.*

GEORGE. It's nice ta see ya Ray.

RAY. It's good ta see you too.

GEORGE. There was rumours flyin' about everywhere sayin' you was nutted off.

RAY. Did ya believe um?

GEORGE. Ah've seen prison fuck up some 'ard cunts in ma time.

RAY. Me mother nutted me off long before prison.

GEORGE. Yeah, you always was a case, no doubt about that. Listen, about the morning, le's jus' keep it to ourselves. Jus' for now.

RAY. No problem.

GEORGE. Maybe we can bring the ol' days back.

RAY. That 'ud be nice.

GEORGE. Are you gonna see ya brother?

RAY. Yeh.

GEORGE *pulls some money from his pocket, hands it to* RAY.

RAY. Woss this?

GEORGE. Pete's givin' it to ya brother.

RAY *takes the money, looks at it, then pockets it.*

RAY. Ah'll see ya in the mornin'.

GEORGE. Take care son.

RAY *exits. Blackout.*

Scene Three

BARRY *and* RAY *enter.* BARRY *stops and watches* RAY *as he walks around the room, looking about him. He stops centre stage.*

BARRY. Left it a bit late, ent ya Ray?

RAY. It's a'right Bal . . . Any tea on the firm?

BARRY. Mum'll be 'ome soon.

RAY. Ain' changed much, 'as it? My bedroom still there?

RAY *pulls out the money and gives it to* BARRY.

BARRY. Woss this?

RAY. It's from Pete, don' ask me.

BARRY *takes the money from* RAY *and puts it in his pocket.*

BARRY. Oh tha's right 'e wants me ta go up Davey's for 'im ta score some brown, ya know Pete owes everyone money.

RAY. Ah wasn'askin' for an explanation, you wanna take gear tha's your problem. When it starts to effect me, ah let ya know.

RAY *takes out some more money and hands it to* BARRY.

RAY. This is for the chain. I got two-eighty for it.

Silence. RAY *stares at the wall.* BARRY *puts the money in his pocket.*

RAY. Wot 'appened ta the crucifix?

BARRY. It's in 'er room.

RAY. Used ta gi' me the creeps that fucker. Ah couldn' sit beneath it, kept thinkin' the cunt was gonna fall on me 'ead.

BARRY. Ah used ta get that feelin' from it.

RAY. Tomorrow.

BARRY. Wot about it?

RAY. I got that drum sorted out.

BARRY. Tomorrow!

RAY. We should get there early. Wossa matter, don' ya wanna do it?

BARRY. Yeh, it's jus' we only wen' out on Monday. I thought we was gonna change the car before we went out again. Ya said yaself we should change the car when it's five missions old.

RAY. It'll be the fifth time tomorrow.

BARRY. Sixth.

RAY. Oh well, woss one extra? After this mission we'll give it a rest for a while. It's the one in Arundel, remember it?

BARRY. Nope.

RAY. Near that castle. Yer know. I was thinkin' we could get some food on the way, stop at the castle 'ave a look roun' get a sense of our 'istory, stack up on the ole culture, an' go off pilligin', like a propah pair of Vikings. What d'ya reckon?

BARRY. Whatever.

RAY. We're gonna eat, so we may as well do it there. It's on the way, the weather man says it's gonna be cloudy but dry.

BARRY. Yeh whatever Ray, I'll pick you up.

RAY. Ah'll meet you 'ere.

BARRY. Wot?

RAY. I meant downstairs . . .

BARRY. A'right.

RAY. Listen Bal, ah know ah've been actin' a right mug, but ya know three years solid is a long time.

BARRY. So ya gonna be sweet from now on?

RAY. Everything's a lot clearer to me now. Ah've put it all in its place. Ah las' few missions 'ave bin mildly successful, ah'm not blamin' anyone for that, before ya jump down me throat. But tomorrow'll be different. Coz ah got a good feeling about this drum . . .

BARRY. Tomorrow then.

RAY. It's took a while, but ah feel all me old instincts comin' back. Ah thought they'd gone for good but naa mate . . . They're stronger than ever. An' it's ya turn ta get the petrol.

BARRY. Sweet.

RAY. It's about a two 'our drive, so make sure ya fill the tank this time.

BARRY. Ah'll see you at the bottom of the stairs then.

RAY *looks about the rooms as he starts to leave. Stops.*

RAY. She knows 'ow to keep a job, don't she? I spose when she retires she can pass the 'ours rememberin' all the tea she's poured, who 'ad milk, who never, who two, who 'ad none. Every time I come back in this 'ouse, it always reminds me of the time I firs' left it. I doubt you'd remember.

BARRY. I doubt I would.

RAY. It was about three in the afternoon. Looked like fuckin' midnight the clouds were so dark. There was me, two social workers an' Mum, drivin' from court. An' they're all tellin' me, I'm not bein' punished an' that Wood'alls isn't a prison, that I would be 'elped. Tha's all they kept sayin'. Over an' over, as the car went further an' further. We was the otherside of Croydon but to me, at that age, it felt like another fuckin' galaxy. I never even thought about runnin' until I was on the pavement an' tear arsin' away. An' them dark clouds opened up an' pissed all over me . . . I thought Mum'd set God on to me. I imagined 'im up there, white beard an' waterin' can, laughin' 'is bollocks off. I dunno why I run. Soon fuckin' realised I 'ad nowhere ta go, 'cept 'ome . . . So with me tail between me legs an' ready ta plead, this is, where I, er . . . I was gonna tell Mum, that I'll change, promise that she'd never 'ave ta get me from the police station again. Beg 'er not ta sen' me away. But she didn' even answer the fuckin' door. The social worker did. I didn' even see Mum. I was starvin' ungry, the cunts wouldn' let me eat. Every stitch o'clothing drenched, even me fuckin' underpants, the cunts wouldn' let me change . . . Ta this day I 'ate the rain. With a fuckin' vengeance.

BARRY. I think I remember, I thought it was a dream . . . I remember you shoutin'an' strugglin' with 'em as ya went down in the lift. Me an' Mum was in 'ere. I think, I dunno. Old memories, it's 'ard ta tell whether they're real or not sometimes ennit?

RAY. That one's real . . . What church she use now?

BARRY. The same one.

RAY. They let 'er back in, 'ow Christian . . . Don' worry Bal, ah'll go before she gets 'ome.

Silence.

God, if ya serving the devil's plate throw some poison on the food . . . Familiar wi' that sayin' Bal?

BARRY. Nope.

RAY. She never said it to you in despair then?

BARRY. Ah never set 'er church alight.

RAY. She said it years before that . . . When ya think about it, an' as ya know ah've 'ad plenny o' time to do that, she don' really believe in God 'erself, well, not the one they preached at Sunday school. That god wouldn' serve the devil, would 'e, Bal?

BARRY. Ah dunno, ah never went to Sunday school..

RAY. Tha's right, ya didn' did ya.

BARRY. She'll be 'ome soon.

RAY. Well tha's between me an'er ennit? I did write to 'er Easter about all this devil's plate bollocks, do ya know if she read it?

BARRY. She never read ya letters.

RAY. Ah only sent the one.

BARRY. Well she never read it.

RAY. She sat me down once, beneath that cross jus' ta tell me, I was the devil 'imself.

BARRY. She's calmed down a lot these days Ray . . .

RAY. If ya servin' the devil's plate, throw some poison on the food . . .

BARRY. Wot time tomorrow?

RAY. About nine. An' don' let me 'ave ta come up an' knock.

BARRY. Ah won't.

RAY *has another look around the room . . . We hear a faint sound of the lift coming up.*

BARRY. That's 'er, Ray.

RAY. I know . . . I'll come earlier nex' time an' you can make me that tea..

BARRY. Yeh definately.

BARRY *watches* RAY *exit, he stands as if to attention in the middle of the room . . . The street door closes. We see* BARRY *physically relax, he pulls a small sheet of foil from his pocket, lights the underside and breathes the fumes coming off the top. We hear the lift door open.* BARRY *screws up the foil and puts it in his pocket. Again he stands in silence. We hear the sounds of the front door opening . . . We can hear* ELLA *shuffling about in the hallway.*

ELLA *enters. She sees* BARRY.

ELLA. What are you standin' up there for?

BARRY. Are you a'right?

ELLA. I'm okay. Shouldn't I be?

BARRY. I was jus' askin'.

ELLA *sits down and stares at* BARRY.

ELLA. Who was that, that jus' left?

BARRY. What?

ELLA. I 'eard our door close as I came up in the lift.

BARRY. I looked out, thought I 'eard someone bibbin'.

Silence. ELLA *stares at* BARRY.

BARRY. Wha's wrong?

ELLA. 'e was just in 'ere wasn'e?

Silence.

ELLA. What did 'e want?

BARRY. 'e was jus' curious, I think.

ELLA. An' was 'is curiosity satisfied when 'e left?

BARRY. I don't know Mum.

ELLA. I didn' think so . . . That blue car downstairs, is that yours?

BARRY. The one jus' by the entrance?

ELLA. Yeh that one . . . It's nice . . .

BARRY. It's sort of mine, I 'aven't paid for it yet.

ELLA. An 'ow're ya gonna do that, when you ain' gotta job?

BARRY. Who says I ain' gotta job?

ELLA. You 'aven't bin to work for weeks.

BARRY. I'm cabbin'.

ELLA. You're a qualified decorator, you don' need ta be cabbin'.

BARRY. There ain' no work about at the moment, I told ya. Fuckin' Marley's not 'ad any work fo' months. It gets like that in the winter. I phone 'im Monday, 'e says phone 'im nex' Monday. I phone 'im nex' Monday, 'e says phone 'im nex' Monday. I feel a mug keep phoning 'im.

ELLA. Yeh . . . They're layin' people off at my place. So I heard.

BARRY. Well they're not gonna lay you off are they?

ELLA. No unfortunately. They don' wanna pay out redundancy money to me, bin there too long fo' that. Mr Peters assured me that I am a very important part of the team. 'e even asked me to start calling him by his Christian name . . . Twenny-five years later.

BARRY. Tha's alright then ennit?

ELLA. You look ill Barry.

BARRY. I'm a'right.

ELLA. You don't look it. Why don't you sit down for a while?

BARRY *goes and sits down. They sit in silence for a moment.*

ELLA. How is ya brother then?

BARRY. What do ya wanna 'ear?

ELLA. Start with the truth an' le's see where it gets us.

BARRY. 'e's alright . . .

ELLA. . . . That it?

BARRY. Yep.

ELLA. I see 'im the other day. 'e was goin' up Brixton Hill in a blue car. Didn't see the driver but I presume it was you . . . Did he pay for the car?

BARRY. 'e gave me some money, said it was a gift an' I put it towards the car.

ELLA. Wha's 'e givin' you money for?

BARRY. 'e jus' said, it was a gift.

ELLA. It's not ya birthday is it?

BARRY. 'e's livin' in a 'ostel in Tulse 'ill, I'll give you the address, you can go an' ask 'im yaself.

ELLA. You shouldda gave it back.

BARRY. 'ow could I do that?

ELLA. Tell 'im ya didn' need it!

I asked 'im once what 'e wunnid to be when 'e grew up. As mums are s'pose' ta do. Ya know 'e didn' even think about it. 'e said, I wanna be a thief. 'e was serious. An' I was fuckin' sorry I asked . . . An' I belted 'im for it . . . Ray wasn' really a dreamer.

BARRY. 'e keeps mentionin' something about a letter.

ELLA. Does 'e?

BARRY. 'e jus' mentioned again, when 'e was 'ere. Did 'e send you a letter?

ELLA. About a year ago.

BARRY. Did ya read it?

Pause.

Mum?

ELLA. No I never, no. Does 'e ask 'ow I am?

BARRY. I spose 'e did in a way, well 'e asked if you was dead yet.

ELLA. Tha's strange, I thought the very same thing today.

BARRY. Don' talk like that Mum.

ELLA. Funny thoughts go through my mind when I'm pushing that tea trolley around . . . All my friends 'ave gone an' left. I shoulda took that redundancy when they offered first time around. I'll always regret that. We got all these fancy names. Hygiene operative, 'ave ya ever 'eard such shit? Refreshments administrator. Who's that spose ta make feel better . . . ? Why did you lie to me about Ray bein' ere?

BARRY. Coz I know 'ow ya get sometimes.

ELLA. You could make excuses for Ray, all ya life before you realise there aint one. 'e's bin that way since the day 'e was born . . . Do you think you could handle prison Barry?

BARRY. I'm not goin' ta prison.

ELLA. All thieves go to prison.

ELLA pulls a cigarette from her bag and lights it.

Ray's more a danger to 'imself than others, dependin' ow close ya get.

BARRY laughs.

You don't think so?

BARRY. I can be fuckin' dangerous too. An' I don' need ta burn down a church ta prove it.

ELLA. Whatever ya doin' with 'im you'd better stop. You'll listen to ya mother won' ya Barry?

BARRY. I don' believe you. At firs' it was like ya wunnid me ta see 'im, ya kept askin' after 'im. Now ya sayin' keep away. Make up ya mind.

ELLA. I don't want you out there burglin' people's 'ouses. I don' like your attitude towards ya brother. You say you could 'andle 'im. You carnt. Many 'ave tried an' failed.

BARRY. I tell ya wot I carn 'andle an' tha's this.

BARRY *rises.*

You only see 'im from in 'ere, from ya own little world. But ya don' see 'im from out there on the streets. 'e maybe some suped up psycho to you, but out there 'e's no more than a village idiot.

ELLA. Whoever told you that? Don' tell me, I don' wanna know. Probably Pete. 'e was always the runt of the litter, that one. But don' be a bigger fool by believin' 'im Barry.

BARRY. Everytime 'e comes out I get this off you.

ELLA. Don't you start accusin' me of things that ain' true. Coz tha's the same bloody thing 'e done. You go out. Get yaself put in prison, or worse.

BARRY. Disownin' me now are ya?

ELLA *stands.*

ELLA. It's you who's doin' the disownin', both of you. I 'eard 'im creepin' down the stairs, jus' before I got in. Now you're about ta walk out. Got some fuckin'ouses to rob 'ave ya?

BARRY *starts walking off.*

You tell Ray I don' wan' 'im in 'ere. I don' want any bloody thieves in this 'ouse!

BARRY *exits.*

Blackout.

Scene Four

GEORGE *sits at the table. He leans back in his seat as* PETE *enters.*

PETE. Sorry ah took so long. 'adda fuckin' nightmare out there.

GEORGE. It took you four an' alf 'ours ta sell a bit o' scrap?

PETE. Ah 'ad ta wait for this mug ta turn up.

GEORGE *rises.*

PETE. Anyone bin in?

GEORGE. Apart from some dodgy lookin' mugs, this one bloke came in three times, fo' fucksake..

PETE. Barry?

GEORGE. Nope.

PETE. Gimme 'is money then.

GEORGE. Ah give it ta Ray ta give to 'im.

PETE. You did what?

GEORGE. 'e was gonna see Barry so I give it to 'im.

PETE. I said give it ta Barry not fuckin' Ray!

GEORGE. Watch ya mouth.

PETE *leans across the table at his father.*

PETE. Two words, a few pages apart in the dictionary but I can't seem ta separate 'em. Cunt an' Dad.

GEORGE. . . . Wot're you up to son?

PETE. Nuffin'. Why should I be up to something?

GEORGE. Maybe ya believe ah can get away with it.

PETE. . . . What the fuck did Ray want?

GEORGE. 'e was lookin' for Barry.

PETE. Did ya talk to 'im?

GEORGE. A bit yeh.

PETE. Ya know Barry's shittin'imself out there?

GEORGE. Why's that then?

PETE. Ray keeps bowlin' about the drums, threatenin' ta burn 'em down.

GEORGE. Well if Barry's that fuckin' scared 'e shouldn' graft with 'im. Ah but then again Barry wouldn' earn 'alf as much as 'e does now.

PETE. Barry's a good drummer mate.

GEORGE. As good as Ray?

PETE. 'e's gettin' there. Ray's still got the talent ta screw any drum 'e likes, but we both know it takes a bit more than that. The geezah 'as definately flipped. All the fuckin' bird 'e's done, it was boun' ta 'appen.

GEORGE. Ain' it time ya spruced this place up a bit, try ta get sum punters back in?

PETE. This is where the money's earnt, at this fuckin' table. Out there's just a front for what goes on in 'ere.

GEORGE. Not much of a front is it? Ar mean if the filth keep seein' the place empty they're gonna ask themselves, 'ow does 'e stay open? Woss 'e up to in there?

PETE *throws a coin onto the table.*

PETE. There ya go, 'ave a game o' pool on ya way out.

GEORGE. Ah'd start takin' me seriously son. I run this place for twelve years ah know what I'm talkin' about.

PETE. If the place was mine I'd do it up. Ya know what ah'd do?

PETE *points at the back wall.*

As far as I'm concerned we don' need that room in there.

GEORGE. The kitchen?

PETE. Like we fuckin' use it.

GEORGE. Carry on.

PETE. We could get a few machines in there, make it into a
little arcade, stick a service 'atch in that wall, that way no
cunts gonna bowl right in, disturbin' business, wantin'
change.

GEORGE. Tha's pretty good son. Wanna lift 'ome?

PETE. No thanks.

GEORGE. Sure?

PETE. No. Yes. 'old on, let me think about it. Course I'm
fuckin' sure.

GEORGE. Jus' offerin'. It soun's good what you was sayin'.
But then you've always sount good, ent ya?

PETE. Well when 'enry sells the place ta me, ah'll stop
talkin'an start doin'.

GEORGE. When 'enry what?

PETE. You 'eard.

GEORGE. You've spoke to 'im about this 'ave ya?

PETE. Ah will do. See 'enry carn' be fucked with this place
any more an' when 'e gets back we're gonna talk. An' tha's
all ah'm sayin'.

GEORGE. Nah ya carnt say too much can ya son?

PETE. Tha's right.

GEORGE. I'll lock up on me way out, shall I?

PETE. Yeh.

> GEORGE *exits . . .* PETE *waits for him to leave. He then*
> *pulls a chair over to the cupboard, climbs up, reaches and*
> *brings his bag of works from the top of the cupboard.*
> BARRY *enters.*

PETE. Thought I 'eard you out there.

> PETE *walks over to the table and empties the bag of works,*
> *syringe, spoon etc onto the table. He sets up a fix*
> *throughout the following dialogue.*

BARRY. Woss ya dad playin' at givin' Ray that money?

PETE. Ah dunno, 'e's goin' senile the ole cunt. What did ya tell Ray?

BARRY. Tol' im I was scorin' some brown fo' you. It was the firs' thing that come into me 'ead. 'e come up the 'ouse, can ya believe that?

PETE. Wot did 'e come up ya 'ouse for?

BARRY. Wants ta go graftin'.

PETE. Again?

BARRY. . . . Yeh. Tomorrow.

PETE. 'e's 'ittin' it a bit 'ard en 'e?

BARRY. Ya got the tackle then?

PETE. 'ad ta wait ages for it.

BARRY. What was that two an'alf for?

PETE. Ya las' mission.

BARRY. Two an' alf!

PETE. It was a monkey but ya owed me two an' alf for the tackle ya bought an'ah 'ad ta take it cos I was gonna score.

BARRY. You said that brooch wassa gran' on its own. Fuckin' thing was covered in ice.

PETE. What tha's called Barry issa cluster, which is loads of tiny almost worthless stones lumped together ta look pukka. Ya carnt sell 'em as items, so what do ya do? Ya break 'em up. Ya still got some ta come for the rings.

BARRY. Well this bit o'brown ya gonna gimme now, ya can take it off the rings money.

PETE. Sweet.

BARRY *removes his belt as he speaks.*

BARRY. Our las' mission right. Ah'm graftin' away, suddenly I start 'earin' this classical music. At firs'ah panic thinkin' they've come 'ome. I go downstairs, 'e's there with a teapot waterin' the fuckin' plants, givin' it like 'e's the lord of the manor . . . I jus' walked out the 'ouse an' sat in the car.

PETE *starts laughing.*

I'm glad you can laugh about it.

PETE. Tha's wot ya gotta do Bal, ya lettin'im get ta ya. Laugh at 'im. Every other cunt does.

BARRY. 'e reckons 'e's gonna be sweet from now on, I tell ya if 'e fucks about tomorrow tha's it . . . Monday mornin' I'm on the phone. I was 'appy decoratin'; a'right the money's shit. But I was fuckin' 'appy.

PETE. You used ta moan like fuck an' remember it's winter. Ya lettin'im wind you up.

PETE *hands* BARRY *the syringe.*

BARRY. Ya dunno 'ow much I need this.

BARRY *looks at the needle in his hand.*

PETE. It don' work by starin' at it.

BARRY. Pete ya gonna 'ave ta do this fo' me. Me 'ands are too shaky.

PETE. Fucksake.

BARRY. I'll lose it all.

PETE *takes the syringe and carefully pushes it into* BARRY*'s arm, he presses the heroin into his vein, then slowly pulls out the needle.* BARRY *sinks back into his seat.*

BARRY. You're a pal Pete.

PETE *straps up his arm.*

PETE. You think you fuckin' need this.

BARRY. . . . Ah'm sure you said ah'd get two gran' . . .

PETE. I said tha's what they're worth.

BARRY. . . . Oh.

PETE *looks over at* BARRY, *who sits with his eyes closed. There is a slight smirk in his face, as he speaks.*

PETE. It's a shame they 'ad ta be broken up . . . It's bollocks 'ow this business runs sometimes.

PETE *injects the heroin into his arm, takes out the needle and throws it on the table. After absorbing the hit he lights a cigarette.* BARRY *sits with his eyes closed.*

PETE. I tell ya, me an' ya brother was pretty close once.

BARRY. Oh yeh.

PETE. Not like that. As pals. Joey come on the firm an' Ray went double weird. I mean 'e must a bin a bit that way but 'e managed to keep it down.

BARRY. Tha's bollocks.

PETE. Ya know Wilson, Marcus an' that?

BARRY. Who?

PETE. Clap'am firm.

BARRY. Yeh.

PETE. They was gonna kick fuck out ya brother an' Joey once. Right naughty firm, propah knife merchants.

PETE *goes into reflective silence.*

BARRY. Wot 'appened?

PETE. I know that firm well an' even though I 'ad the 'ump with ya brother an' Joey, ah wasn' gonna stan' there an' let 'em cop a beatin'. I ain' like that, they're off the manna an' that means something to me. It's a shame other bods don't see it the same way . . . Didn' thank me or nuffin' ya brother.

BARRY. Bollocks.

PETE. But it doesn' matter Barry, tha's wot ah'm tryin' ta tell ya . . . Ray's a cunt but you can live wi' that . . . 'e'll fin' another driver in no time; ya fuck 'im off.

BARRY. Yeh.

PETE. 'ave a good think about it firs'. Eight 'ours a day, six
days a week, Marley gettin, on ya case, Migrain's off the
fuckin' gloss.

BARRY *does not answer.*

PETE. Pukka gear, eh.

BARRY. Yeh . . . I sometimes wonder something.

PETE. . . . Wot?

BARRY. . . . Wot?

PETE. You sometimes wonder something.

BARRY. Oh . . . What Ray an' Joey got up to in the drums?

PETE. Them sort o' thoughts can seriously damage ya buzz . . .

Blackout.

ACT TWO

Scene One

The lights come up on the lounge of a country manor house.
Two armchairs sit centre stage. RAY enters with a tray of tea.
He places the tray on a small coffee table that sits between the
two chairs. He peels off his bright pink washing-up gloves,
pockets them. From another pocket he pulls out a small bag
of weed. He sits in one of the chairs, picks up a pipe from the
table and starts packing it with weed, sticks the pipe in his
mouth and lights it. He puffs on it for a while, inhales deeply,
then blows a stream of smoke into the air. He puts down the
pipe and pours himself a cup of tea . . . He sips.

RAY. Ahh, ma fuckin' word tha's lovely.

He takes another sip and savours the taste. He gets up from
the chair and exits the room. He enters a few moments later,
carrying a tin of tea and drops it into his bag. He sits and
takes another sip of his tea.

RAY. Unfuckin' real that.

He picks up the pipe.

BARRY *enters, stops. He watches RAY as he lights the*
pipe. Small clouds of smoke drift towards the ceiling.

RAY. Wot kept ya?

BARRY. Ah thought you weren' gonna fuck about any more?

RAY. Ah finished down 'ere so ah thought ah'd make a pot o'
rosy. Tell ya wot mate, ah've 'it the fuckin' jackpot down
'ere.

BARRY. Wot 'ave ya got?

RAY *pulls the tin of tea from the bag, hands it to BARRY,*
who studies it.

RAY. Open it then.

BARRY *opens the tin, looks inside.*

BARRY. It's tea?

RAY. Smell it.

BARRY *puts the lid back on the tea and hands it back to* RAY.

BARRY. Wot the fuck ya playin' at Ray?

RAY. Ah say one thing for the upper classes, they know their fuckin' tea. Sit down, ah'll pour you a cup.

BARRY. Ah don' want one . . . If ya finished le's go.

RAY. Ah jus' poured it.

BARRY. Ah ain' talkin' about the fuckin' tea!

RAY. The company 'as decided ta call a meetin', it's laid on tea an' biscuits, in a cosy surround, comfy chairs and a welcoming smile from the managin' director.

RAY *turns and smiles at* BARRY.

BARRY. Ah'll fuckin' leave ya Ray, ah swear ta God.

RAY. Don' swear at 'im, 'e's got enough on 'is plate, with all us devils runnin' aroun'.

BARRY. Ah ain'avin' this bollox t'day.

BARRY *turns and starts to walk away.*

RAY. Gimme one minute.

BARRY *turns and looks at his watch.*

BARRY. Ya time starts now.

RAY. Ya remember as we was walkin' towards the drum, ah asked you ta go to the car an' get me gloves?

RAY *picks up his tea.*

RAY. What did you do? You threw the car keys at me an' tol' me ta get 'em meself . . . weren' very nice was it?

Pause. RAY *sips his tea.*

RAY. Ah got an announcement ta make Bal . . . . Barry.

BARRY. Wot fo' fucksake!

RAY. This is me las' mission an'ah wanna make the most of it.

BARRY. By gettin' us both banged up?

RAY. 'ave ya bin banged up Bal?

BARRY. Wot does it fuckin' matter . . .

Silence.

Ya know I 'aven't!

RAY. Bin chored?

BARRY. Yeh.

RAY. Let me guess. T.D.A.?

BARRY. Yeh.

RAY. Wot did ya steal?

BARRY. A car.

RAY. Yeh, 'eard it was a milk float.

BARRY. If ya fuckin' know, wot're ya askin' me for?

RAY. 'ow did they catch ya?

BARRY. It was the others that stole it an' got it stuck on the grass be'ind our block. They asked me ta 'elp 'um. I wasn' gonna start pushin' the thing through the mud, so I said I'd drive. Nex' thing I know this gavva's draggin' me about by me fuckin' ear. The others 'ad fucked off without warnin' me. Said they tried. I was on me way to the shop ta buy some milk, tha's the bollocks thing about it.

RAY. What did Mum say?

BARRY. Gimme the silent treatment. Fuckin' ear 'urt fo' months.

RAY. Frankie Fraser's got nothin' on you 'as 'e?

BARRY. Jus'cos you've bin inside all ya life don' make you anything. No, sorry, I'm wrong, it does, it makes you a mug.

RAY. Don' I fuckin' know it . . . 'ave a seat Bal.

BARRY. Ah'm a'right standin'.

RAY takes another sip of his tea.

RAY. Ah can't say enough about this tea yer know. Ah take it without milk now. Ah 'ad no choice inside, but ah got used to it. Now ya put milk anywhere near me tea ah'll go mad, carnt stan' the stuff. On its own ah love it, but not in me fuckin' tea.

BARRY. Ah take it the meeting's started?

Silence.

For fucksake.

BARRY slowly walks over to the chair and sits. RAY leans over and pours him a cup of tea.

RAY. Milk?

BARRY. If ya like.

RAY. It ruins it yer know.

BARRY. Ah sat down ta 'ear you out, keep ya fuckin' tea an' say ya piece.

RAY. Why are you out 'ere with me Barry?

BARRY. For the fuckin' life of me I don' know.

RAY. You made the choice.

BARRY. Well I didn' think I'd 'ave ta put up with all this bollocks, did I.

RAY. Thinkin's not one o'ya strong points is it Barry . . . ?

RAY sips his tea.

Ya know these rich bods would never invite us into their 'ouses, not unless it was ta serve 'em. So you jus' think. Think wot they'd do, if they foun' a pair o' South London slum 'eads like us, bowlin' about, takin' liberties with their tea? They'd weigh us off a fuckin' lump, first offence or not. They'd probably even know the judge that sentenced us.

BARRY. Tha's jus' wot I wanna 'ear ennit Ray?

RAY. The fact that ya lookin' a two, ya get chored. No fuckin' bail. Musta crossed ya min' at some point over the las' month?

BARRY. You mus' be lookin' at four then.

RAY. Maybe five. That las' sentence 'as put a severe dent in me career prospects, I must admit. Tha's wot 'appens when ya graft with amateurs. Ya never really got ta know Joey did ya?

BARRY. Knew enough.

RAY. Woss enough?

BARRY. Thought 'e was 'ard but 'e was just a wanker.

RAY. You made that assumption under no influence whatsoever?

BARRY. Yes your fuckin'onour.

RAY. Didn' know 'im that well. Ah see some similarities between ya both.

BARRY. Ah'm nuffin' like 'im. Are we in the meetin' now?

RAY. Yeh. In what way are ya nuffin' like 'im?

BARRY. I never got you banged up fo' three years, for one. An' for two I'm not splattered all over Streat'am 'igh Road.

RAY *laughs.*

RAY. Ya definately got the same sense of 'umour. Cos you can be a right funny at times Bal.

BARRY. Wot the fuck are you goin' on about?

RAY. All in good time . . . Bro . . .

BARRY. I don' see us doin' anything 'ere we carn't do in the car.

RAY. Ah can never think properly in the car.

BARRY. Wot about a prison cell?

RAY. What about it? Don' worry Bal, if they come in the front way, we'll go out the back. Ah'd love ta see what you'd do if it came on top.

BARRY. Ah'd run.

RAY. When ya can walk.

BARRY. Ah but you've jus' done three years ent ya Ray? Ya a right 'ard cunt now.

RAY. Run all the way back ta london would ya?

BARRY. Your fuckin' enjoyin' this ent ya?

RAY. . . . Ah am as it goes. 'ow did ya do upstairs?

BARRY *takes a pouch out of his pocket and throws it on the table.*

BARRY. See for yaself.

RAY. You do wanna stay 'ere all day don't ya?

BARRY. It's written all over me face ennit?

RAY. 'ow long ya bin on the gear Bal?

BARRY. None o'ya fuckin' business.

RAY. Are you jus' smokin' or are ya jackin' up now?

BARRY *jumps up from his seat.*

BARRY. A'right cunt, you've 'ad ya say. Now it's ma turn.

RAY. Tha's what this meetin's all about.

BARRY. If ya think ya can spend three years inside, come out an' treat me like ya little brother, ya wrong! Ah jack up in me fuckin' eyeballs, me bollox the works. Ah don' give a shit where ah stick the needle an'ah don' give a fuck what you think!

Pause as RAY sips his tea.

RAY. Ah find anger ta be one of the most 'onest emotions, don't you?

BARRY. Ya go on about Mum an'ow fuckin' cruel she was, wantin' every cunt's sympathy! But you don' know the 'alf of it.

RAY. Well tell me Bal.

BARRY. Where was you when Mum was in 'ospital? Tell me that?

RAY. I didn' even know she was in 'ospital.

BARRY. Didn' fuckin' care much either.

RAY. Wot was she in for?

BARRY. Nervous exhaustion . . . She 'adda breakdown. At work . . . In front of all the fuckin' people . . . I came 'ome from school ta be tol' I'll be livin' with Ted an' Joan the neighbours, 'ave you ever bin in their 'ouse!? Stinks like a fuckin' zoo!

RAY. When was this?

BARRY. Like you care.

RAY. When was this!?

BARRY. I was in the third year! . . . She was only gone a couple o' days . . . She wunnid ta go back ta work straight away, ya know wot Mum's like, but they wouldn' let 'er.

RAY. Was that the time ya wen' on 'oliday?

BARRY. If ya call two weeks at Brighton in the pissin' rain a 'oliday, yeh.

RAY. Was she better after the 'oliday?

BARRY. Yeh.

RAY. Well tha's the main thing ennit? Not the fact that nex' door stink or Brighton pissed down. But that Mum was a'right.

BARRY. Don' try an' turn it roun' on me! It was you that put 'er in 'ospital! Not fuckin' me! YOU!

They both sit in silence. RAY *pours himself some more tea.*

RAY. George gave me breakfas' this mornin'.

BARRY. Yeh, tha's nice.

RAY. Nice?

BARRY. 'e never gives breakfas' ta anyone else. Even Pete 'as ta pay.

RAY. Yeh well 'e never built that cafe off the back of Pete. 'e built it off the back o' me. Sa when ya think about it breakfas' is a fuckin' piss take.

BARRY. Maybe you should tell 'im that.

RAY. Firs' thing firs'. I built everything that family owns, includin' Master 'enry. Pete's gotta be a dick'ead en 'e? Ah mean when ya young ya look up ta ya older brother, it's natural. But as ya get older, things start ta even out a bit. 'enry says jump an' Pete flies off the face of the earth. Propah wanker . . . All that about 'ow 'e rowed them bods, when they robbed 'im. Did you believe that?

BARRY. No reason not to.

RAY. It weren' three bods, it was two an' Pete sat in 'is chair tremblin' so much it measured on the richter scale. 'e's not jus' ya average plastic gangster, our Pete, nah, 'e reigns supreme over all.

BARRY. You set 'im up?

RAY. And? . . .

BARRY *shakes his head in dismay.*

RAY. See 'im wi' that knife . . . Fuckin'don of Legoland, the cunt . . .

RAY *lights the pipe again, he inhales, closes his eyes and lets the smoke drift out of his mouth.*

. . . Ya know when I first asked you if ya wannid ta graft? You said yes like you was waitin' for the question.

BARRY. Shouldn'ave asked if it bothered ya.

RAY. You kept tellin' me ya 'ad no work . . . Nex' thing Pete's set up a car an' we're flyin' down the A217. Ya don' know Pete. You don' know that fuckin' geezah at all.

BARRY. Sa why do you use 'im then Ray, if 'e's such a wanker?

RAY. George can offload anything, not jus' tom, I'm talkin', paintin's, antiques, the lot. Good contacts . . . Naturally when the son takes over, the ole man passes these contacts on to 'im.

RAY *shakes his head.*

RAY. An' to my fuckin'orror I fin' out from George that this ain' so. But other than that I do know Pete . . . (*Impersonates* PETE.) A'right Bal 'ow ya doin', me an' ya brother go way back. Come an'ave a game o'pool any time ya want mate' . . . (*Ends impersonation.*) Ya go down, 'ave a spliff, start talkin', made ya feel like ya one of the boys, 'e'll look after ya. So on an' so on. Tell me that ain' ow it 'appened?

BARRY. That ain'ow it 'appened.

RAY. Bollocks . . . So ya think Pete's up front then? Wot ya see is wot ya get yeh?

BARRY. Couldn' give a fuck.

RAY. Well start to Bal, coz ah wanna go 'ome!

BARRY. 'e's sweet wi'me.

RAY. Thick as shit.

BARRY. Jus' like me brother!

RAY. Ya don' love ya brother do ya Bal?

BARRY. Ey?

RAY. Wossamatter, the question too 'ard for ya?

BARRY. Na it's fuckin' easy, ah 'ate ya . . . Ya got the fuckin' front ta go on about bein' professional, tell me woss professional about this? 'oldin' me in this 'ouse? This ain' fuckin' sane. You aint!

RAY. Oh an' you know about bein' sane do ya?

BARRY. A lot more than you fuckin' do.

RAY. What is it then? Sayin' nish when some cunt shits on ya?
Puttin' ya faith in something unseen? If ya ever see a bit o'
sane, show us, coz I'd love ta see wot the cunt looks like . . .

BARRY. Nuffin' like you tha's for sure.

RAY. Let me tell ya about this fraggle I met, reminded me a bit
of you. 'e was a skag'ead like yaself. On 'is firs sentence.
Couldn'andle it. I'd 'ear'im nex'door every fuckin'night
cryin' 'is self ta sleep . . . It came as a relief when 'e cut
'is wrists, I must admit. An' 'e done 'em an'all, silly cunt
nearly chopped 'is fuckin'and off. An'e was one o'many.
I swear blind they were bringin' the cunts in on a conveyor
belt. An' certifieds like meself 'ave ta lie in our peters
an'listen ta these pricks cryin' for their mothers. They
couldda bin insane, I dunno. The situation they foun'
themselves in was. But when ya look into the eyes of the
doctors an' screws, raw fuckin' insanity. Good 'as waved the
white flag of surrender while evil pins ya to the floor an'
sticks a needle up ya arse. You'd probably like that . . .

BARRY *looks at the floor and does not respond.*

Patient 'as withdrawn into 'imself . . . Possible suicide
risk . . . Dose 'im with serum . . . This one always cracks
me up. Patient was angry, for no conceivable fuckin' reason!
They got reports datin' back ta when Dad died. They know
it all these cunts.

RAY *takes a ready rolled spliff from his pocket and lights it.
He inhales deeply.*

I 'aven't quite got the complete picture on insanity, but
ah'm gettin there. This geezah, Fieldman used ta run Wood
'alls 'e wrote at the end of 'is report, 'I have one word to
describe Ray. Disturbed.' 'e was spot on . . . There's no
two ways about it. But then 'avin' an evil barsted like 'im
carin' for ya was pretty fuckin' disturbin' . . . 'e would stan'
there . . . an' watch. (*Lights spliff.*) . . . I used ta love
freakin' the cunts out. Next meetin' started well, then

patient began to speak in an incoherent manner of a . . .
dark nature? What did they expect, the soun' of fuckin'
music? After climbin' about on the furniture, Patient ended
meetin' by layin' on the table in a foetal position suckin' is
thumb. Refer to psychiatric unit. Shouldda known better,
insanity 'as no sense of 'umour. Ya wake up lyin' in ya own
shit an' piss, not knowin' where the fuck you are, prayin'
it's a prison.

RAY *relights his spliff.*

. . . That ya wouldn' like.

BARRY. It's not gonna 'appen ta me is it?

RAY. Nah you'll be too busy 'ackin' up ya wrists.

BARRY. No way.

RAY. Keepin' us all awake at nights. (*Impersonates* BARRY
crying.) *Mummy help me, Mummy I'm dyin', Mummy.*

BARRY. Jus' coz you cracked up! Coz you couldn' 'andle the
bird! Don' mean ya should start takin' it out on me!

RAY. I don' ave ta be in prison ta suffer severe bouts of
'onesty . . .

RAY *takes another puff on his spliff.*

Thanks for listenin' Bal, it's not often I get ta talk about
these things, I appreciate it, I really fuckin' do.

BARRY. Don' mention it.

RAY. Nah ah should mention it, I mean ya know all this don't
ya? You've 'eard the rumours . . .

BARRY. I've 'eard.

RAY. An' all the time we've spent together over the las' month,
ya never once thought ta ask me about it?

BARRY. Ah didn' fuckin' need to.

RAY. Wot about the other one?

BARRY. Other what?

RAY. Rumour. About me an' Joey?

BARRY. Ah'm not with ya.

RAY. Yes you are . . . Don' ya ever wonder wot we used ta get up to in the drums . . . ? Wanna go 'ome t'day or wot?

BARRY. Ya a pair o'fuckin'nonces a'right!

RAY. Ah don' paint a pretty picture in that 'ead of yours, do I? . . . Ya ready.

BARRY jumps up from his chair.

RAY. Oh, one more thing.

RAY picks up the pouch from the table.

Is this the tom ya put down ya bollox?

BARRY. Wot?

RAY. You 'eard.

BARRY. You are off ya fuckin' nut mate.

RAY. That wasn't the question I asked . . .

BARRY. Well it's the answer ya gonna get from now on.

RAY. Due to lack of earnin's, ah thought ah'd come up stairs wi' you today, make sure you was doin' ya job properly. 'ave ya bin doin' it from the beginning?

BARRY. Ah don' give a shit about the keys. Ah'd rather walk than share a car wi' you.

BARRY starts to walk away.

RAY. You take another STEP AH FUCKIN' DARE YA!

BARRY stops dead in his tracks.

RAY. If ya don' get that tom out an'on the table ah'm gonna get it meself! Ah see ya Bal. Ya sat on the bed, sorted out which ones ya wunnid an'stuck um down ya bollox. Now, if ah 'ave ta get um meself, ah might pull out the wrong bag!

BARRY. Why're ya doin' this Ray . . . ?

RAY. Ya're in deep enough as it is Barry.

BARRY *looks to the ceiling as if in prayer . . . He walks over to* RAY, *producing a small pouch from down his trousers. He puts it on the table and stands back . . .* RAY *picks up the pouch, rises and goes to the front of the stage. He takes a ring from the bag and studies it.*

BARRY. Ah never meant to Ray.

RAY. Shut ya fuckin' mouth an' si' down.

BARRY *remains still.*

BARRY. Le's sort this out at 'ome Ray.

RAY. SIT IN THE FUCKIN' CHAIR!

BARRY *sits down.* RAY *pulls another ring from the pouch and studies it.*

RAY. Joey done the same thing. So I jus' dunnit it back. Tha's 'ow come they foun' the egg. Tha's 'ow come I do three years.

RAY *holds the ring, on the tip of his finger, to the light.*

Cut ta perfection. Look at the way it jus' sprays the light out. Like little sunrays. Pete wouldda 'ad a right touch.

RAY *drops the ring back into the pouch and tucks it into his jacket pocket.*

BARRY. Ah'll pay ya back Ray . . . Ah swear ta ya, ah swear, on our nex' few missions everything we earn is yours . . .

RAY *lights his spliff.*

Ya right about Pete. Dead fuckin' right . . . 'e's made a right mug outa me. But I've only jus' met the geezah en' I? 'e tol' me you was doin' the same an' takin' ya stuff to George. The gear as well, that was, sort o' made me believe wot 'e was sayin'. I dunno 'ow things go in this game Ray . . .

RAY. Pete don' mean nuffin' ta me . . .

BARRY. Mum she says things but deep down ah know she don' mean 'em. If I talk to 'er. Maybe we could sort things out a bit.

Silence . . .

RAY. You shouldn'ave stolen from me Barry.

RAY *throws the spliff down, turns and walks towards*
BARRY. *He walks around the back of* BARRY.

BARRY (*turning towards* RAY). Pete twisted me fuckin'ead
up!

RAY *grabs the back of the chair and wrenches it backwards*
onto the floor, where he begins to punch BARRY. RAY
turns the unconscious BARRY *around and throws his head*
over the upturned chair. Blood drips from his face.

RAY. Every drop of blood in your body is pure evil. Tha's wot
she'd say.

RAY *undoes* BARRY*'s trousers.*

The day I was christened I screamed down the church!

RAY *wrenches* BARRY*'s trousers down.*

An' she knew it then!

RAY *unfastens his own trousers.*

That she'd sporned the fuckin' devil!

RAY *leans over and holds* BARRY*'s head down with one*
hand.

An' like a preacher to 'is flock ah'm gonna put the fucker in
you.

RAY *bends over* BARRY *and thrusts into him.* BARRY
starts to regain his senses. RAY *thrusts again.* BARRY
realises what is happening to him and starts to struggle.
RAY *pulls away. In a blind panic,* BARRY *tries to get up*
off the floor, away from RAY *and pull his trousers up. He*
stumbles and falls, ending up on his back centre stage.
He pulls up his trousers. He looks at RAY, *an expression*
of shock and horror on his face.

RAY *stands doing up his trousers, looking back at* BARRY,
his expression blank.

Silence . . . Just the sound of BARRY*'s breathing.*

BARRY *stiffens as* RAY *walks around the chair to the table. Covering his hands with the cuff of his coat, he picks up the teapot and wipes the handle. He does the same with the pipe and the cup. He picks up the bag and hangs it around his shoulder. He does not look at* BARRY *as he exits.*

We hear the front door slam shut. BARRY *curls up into a ball and starts sobbing.*

We hear the sound of a car engine coming to life. Then a crude crunching sound as RAY *puts the car into gear. We hear the tyres spin on the gravel drive, the car hit some dustbins and stall. The car starts again, after another wheel-spin, we hear it drive off.*

What starts as a low whine from the pit of BARRY*'s stomach, ends as a piercing cry from his mouth.*

Blackout.

Scene Two

GEORGE *and* PETE *sit around the table. In front of* GEORGE *stands a bottle of whiskey and a glass, half full.* GEORGE *starts to cough, he sips some whiskey and puffs on his cigarette. His coughing dies down.* PETE *looks at him in disgust.*

PETE. Ya need more of what makes ya cough ta stop ya coughin'.

GEORGE. Well observed son.

GEORGE *takes another sip of his whiskey.*

GEORGE. You used ta like a tipple y'self.

PETE. An' ah don' any more, well observed Dad.

GEORGE. You'd filla glass, smoke a joint an' get totally blotto. Then suddenly ya stopped. Now tha's will power for ya.

PETE. Proud 'o me are ya?

GEORGE. Not at all.

PETE. Nah, ya not beamin'. When ya proud ya eyes sparkle. Ya chest puffs out.

GEORGE. When was that then?

PETE. When 'enry used ta play football. You'd stan' there all puffed out. 'e's gonna be the nex' Peter Osgood, ma son. The joke is ya knew nuffin' about the game.

GEORGE. 'e was a good player. Couldda bin a pro. Broke me fuckin'eart when 'e gave it up.

PETE. Ever thought ta ask why 'e gave it up?

GEORGE. 'e gave it up when ya mum died. 'e lost all 'eart fo' the game after that.

PETE. Bollox. 'e was sick o' you standin' on the touch line shoutin' crap, coz ya never 'adda clue. 'e was sick of the other players laughin' at ya. 'e never lost 'is 'eart, you stole it from 'im.

GEORGE *puts out his cigarette and immediately lights another. He takes a sip of his whiskey.*

PETE. If ya gonna sulk piss off 'ome an' do it.

GEORGE. When you married that woman an' 'ad my beautiful gran'daughter, you made me very proud. Marie's a special woman.

PETE. Don' worry about Marie, she gets looked after. Anyway I don' really wanna 'ear it. I got fuckin' work to do this evenin' an' to be 'onest ah'd rather you weren'ere.

PETE *looks at his watch.*

GEORGE. Late ent they?

PETE. Nah.

GEORGE. Maybe they've gone elsewhere. If they 'ad any sense tha's what they'd do.

PETE. An' where will they go? You?

GEORGE. When ah'm sittin' right 'ere?

PETE. Ah know ya fuckin' game.

GEORGE. Only cos ya played it son.

PETE. Ah sussed you.

GEORGE. What 'ave ya sussed?

PETE. You right out. Don' think, all the time you've bin nosin' aroun'asn' gone unnoticed. Ya after me fuckin' drummers. Ray gets out an' cash registers start ringin' in ya 'ead. But me an' 'enry both know ya past it.

GEORGE. Ah told ya not ta speak for ya brother.

PETE. Jus' recitin' back to you what we discussed today.

GEORGE. Spoken to 'im 'ave ya?

PETE. Called 'im on 'is mobile. 'e tol' me ta tell you ta fuck off.

GEORGE. 'e said that did 'e?

PETE. Sorry ta break it to ya like that.

GEORGE *stands. He takes a letter from his pocket, slowly unfolds it and lays it on the table in front of* PETE.

PETE. Woss this?

GEORGE. Read it.

Silence as PETE *reads the letter.*

GEORGE. Ma signiture jus' beneath 'enry's should interest you.

PETE *screws up the letter and throws it at* GEORGE.

PETE. Fuckin' worthless.

GEORGE. Yep. The original's tucked away in me safe.

GEORGE *brushes the crumpled letter onto the floor.*

PETE. We'll see about this when 'enry gets back.

GEORGE. Ah thought 'e wouldda mentioned it, when ya spoke to 'im.

PETE. 'enry wouldn't let ya run this place, ya an old man, bods'll take the piss out a ya.

GEORGE. You obviously didn' read the deeds properly. Ah'm not gonna run the place, ah fuckin' own it. Sorry ta break it to ya like that.

Pause as GEORGE *sips his whiskey.*

Ah must admit ah did like wot ya said about turnin' the kitchen into an arcade. Ah'm definately gonna give that some serious thought.

PETE *jumps up from his seat, digs his hands into his pocket.*

PETE. If ya want the fuckin' place!

As PETE *rips the keys from his pocket and throws them down, a small wrap of heroin falls onto the table.*

PETE. You can fuckin'ave it! I'll see 'enry when 'e gets back.

GEORGE *looks at the wrap of heroin.* PETE *follows his gaze and also sees it. They both go for it at the same time.* GEORGE *gets there first,* PETE*'s hand landing on top.*

Silence.

GEORGE. Ya gonna let go o' me 'and?

PETE *lets go.* GEORGE *starts to unfold the wrap.*

GEORGE. All that trouble we went to.

PETE. Ah didn' tell ya to.

GEORGE. No ya fuckin' begged us. Do ya still wanna wait fo' 'enry ta get back?

GEORGE *lays the open wrap on the table.*

PETE. Ah got nish ta 'ide. It's Barry's.

GEORGE. To the bitter end ya go. We spent three gran' keepin' you in that re'ab.

PETE. Ya never paid a penny.

GEORGE. Who paid ya mortgage?

PETE. Ah'll pay ya back don' worry.

GEORGE. Who kept ya wife an' kid, while you were there?

PETE. It was the missus. Marie told ya.

GEORGE. Women always know what ya up to. They always know when they're bein' cheated on. Most push it to the back of their mind an' say nish. Some don't. Marie comes in the some section. 'ow the fuck did you expect ta run aroun' the streets, with all these little trollops followin' ya an' not get captured? Ya got junkies knockin' on ya door. Birds ringin' ya at all 'ours. She never came ta me nahh, I wish she did, things wouldda bin a lot easier. She went straight to 'enry. Ya jus' lucky I foun' 'im before 'e foun' you.

PETE. The cunt.

GEORGE. She says you've bin back on it a year, which means you were only out of that re'ab a couple o' months. We don' feel let down, son, we feel we've 'ad the piss taken . . . I 'ad to force 'enry onto that train cos 'e wunnid to deal with it 'imself.

PETE. Ah spose ya want me thanks?

GEORGE. No, cos ah dunnit fo' 'enry.

PETE. Managed ta get ya name on the deeds firs'.

GEORGE *picks up the heroin, as he speaks, bits of heroin fall from the wrap, causing* PETE *obvious anxiety.*

GEORGE. This is a family business under our family's name. Ya don'sell skag from 'ere. If you wanna go down, then go. Don' drag us with ya. You can keep the keys fo' tonight, deal wi' ya drummers. Ah'm pickin' 'enry up from the station in the mornin'.

PETE. Then what?

GEORGE. Jus' disappear son.

GEORGE *looks at the heroin in his hand.*

PETE. There's two 'undred quids worth of gear there Dad.

GEORGE *suddenly blows the heroin all over the table.*
PETE *grips his head in disbelief.* GEORGE *screws up the
wrap and throws it at* PETE, *hitting him in the face.*
GEORGE *gets up from his seat.* PETE *stares at the table,
still in a state of shock.*

GEORGE. Ya mother'd turn in 'er grave.

PETE *suddenly swings for* GEORGE, *who steps out the
way, grabs* PETE*'s arm, bends it up behind his back and
slams him face down across the table.*

GEORGE. We was there for ya las' time, this time ya on ya
own.

GEORGE *lets* PETE *go. He picks up his cigarettes and
bottle of whiskey, has one last glance at his son.*

GEORGE. By the way, Marie's left ya.

GEORGE *exits . . .*

PETE *starts trying to save some of the heroin that is spread
across the table-cloth.*

RAY *appears beyond the doorway, silently he watches*
PETE.

Finding it difficult to retrieve his gear, PETE *almost
bursts into tears. He curses his father while scraping and
picking . . . He then drags a chair across the room to the
cupboard.* RAY *enters and sits silently at the table, he leans
over and looks at the wrap of heroin.* PETE *gets down from
the cupboard, turns and is startled when he sees* RAY.

RAY. A'right mate?

PETE. Fo'fucksake Ray!

RAY. Didn' mean ta scare ya Pete. Two 'undred quids worth o'
gear an' tha's all ya salvaged. Ya mus' be gutted mate?

PETE. Plenny more where that came from.

PETE *prepares a fix throughout the following dialogue.*

RAY. Are ya gonna jack up?

PETE. Got a problem wi' that?

RAY. Not at all.

PETE. Where's Barry?

RAY. Good fuckin' question . . .

PETE. Well?

RAY. Ah am thank you.

PETE. Where's Barry yer cunt?

RAY. Well ah was too busy gettin' away, didn' see where 'e went.

PETE. Ya left 'im?

RAY. Never 'ad much fuckin' choice Pete. Anyway a bit o'bird'll do 'im good . . .

PETE. 'ow long was ya outside?

RAY. Fuckin' ages. Ah thought the ole man was never gonna piss off. Ah wouldda jus' bowled in sooner but it seemed you two needed ta talk.

PETE. We always fall out. Nuffin' new.

RAY. That wasn' your face I 'eard knockin' against the table was it?

RAY pulls out a half smoked spliff and lights it.

PETE. It was a whiskey bottle.

RAY. Didn' soun' like it.

PETE. I picked it up ta 'it 'im, realised wot I was doin' an' throw it down on the table.

RAY. An' this always 'appens, yeh?

Pause as PETE stops what he is doing and looks at RAY.

PETE. Don' take the piss outta me Ray.

RAY. Wot?

PETE get backs to setting up his fix.

RAY. Ah realised something today. Ah need a woman.

PETE. Too much wankin' makin' ya dick sore?

RAY. Ya ain' got any trollops 'angin'aroun'ave ya?

PETE. Carn 'elp ya.

RAY. Not let Maureen off 'er leash yet then?

PETE. Nope.

RAY. Wot not even ta cock 'er leg up a lamp post?

PETE. Good enough for ya now is she?

RAY. Jus' shows ya the depths of depravity a man stoops to, when 'e's jus' got out of prison.

PETE. Ya've bin out over a month, if ya carn fin' a fuck, give up now mate.

RAY. I'm askin' about Maureen when Marie's free now, ent she?

PETE *concentrates on filling the needle.*

RAY. So the ole man's really bootin' ya out? It's jus' one thing after another ennit. Ya duck the left an'a right does ya on the chops. Ah fuckin' know about it mate. But look on the bright side, least ya won' 'ave ta clean out that bog.

PETE *straps up his arm and taps up a vein. He is about to inject, when he feels* RAY *watching him. He stops and looks at him.*

PETE. Do ya 'ave ta watch?

RAY. Never seen someone jack up before.

PETE *moves around in his seat until his back is facing* RAY. RAY *leans under the table and gets the knife.*

RAY. Get it up there son!

RAY *takes the knife from beneath the table.* PETE *turns back around, throws the syringe onto the table and sinks back into his seat.*

PETE. Be with ya in a minute.

RAY. You take ya time.

> RAY *lights his spliff. Silence . . .*

PETE. 'ow did you get 'ome?

RAY. I started off by car, then . . . well I was on foot for a few miles. Then train, then bus. An'ere I am.

PETE. You an' cars don' exactly mix ey?

RAY. We did for a few miles.

PETE. And?

RAY. We fell out. This lovely lookin' woman flew past, callin' me a wanker. I dunno what I done, but she 'ad the right 'ump. Ya don' need that when ya tryin' ta concentrate.

PETE. Ya musta cut 'er up.

RAY. Nah bollocks, road rage, ah read about it inside.

PETE. She ain' gonna go mad for nish.

RAY. A'right I nudged 'er a bit on a roundabout.

PETE. . . . Shall ah call ya Mister O'Neal or jus' Ryan from now on?

RAY. Ah was tryin' ta light me spliff. Barry always made smokin'an' drivin' look easy.

PETE. You don' seem too concerned about ya brother.

RAY. Ah'm not in the least bit concerned about me brother. You do seem quite concerned?

PETE. Ah am. Barry's a mate.

RAY. No such thing as mates in this business.

PETE. Well ah made an exception with Barry.

RAY. Why's that then?

PETE. Cos ah like the geezah.

RAY. An' 'e likes you too.

PETE. Let's sort out this tom, I got some thinkin' ta do.

RAY. Sure ya got the money?

PETE. I got the money.

RAY. Here?

PETE. Yeh.

RAY. I gotta ask. I mean ya dad an' 'enry's not fundin' ya any
more are they?

*PETE takes out a wad of notes from his pocket and slams it
on the table.*

PETE. I don' fuckin' need 'enry.

RAY. Tell ya what before we start . . .

RAY reaches into his bag and pulls out the tin of tea.

Smell that for a pot o' rosy. Propah English tea from India,
better than that stewed shit ya Dad brews in the cafe.

PETE takes the tin and smells.

PETE. Fuckin' poof's tea.

*RAY takes the bundle of cash, rises from his chair and puts
it in his pocket. PETE watches him, stunned. His hand goes
under the table for his knife. When he cannot feel it, he
ducks underneath to look. RAY pulls the knife from his
coat. PETE slowly looks up.*

RAY. I spent 'alf this bright winter's day wonderin'ow I was
gonna kill ya. Thoughts of torture an' everything. Then I
thought nahh, leave the mug to 'imself.

PETE. Ya fuckin'silly if ya think you can get away with this.

RAY. I didn' expect any gratitude for lettin'ya live. But all
things considered you should be grateful.

PETE. Whatever Barry's done ain'got nuffin'ta do wi' me.

RAY. Why, wha's Barry done then . . . ?

PETE. Tha's all the money I got Ray . . .

RAY. Had . . . Bet I've right fucked up ya buzz ey . . . ?

PETE. 'enry's gonna be well pissed off.

RAY I've no doubt.

PETE. 'e's still me bruvvah, despite wot me ole man says. 'e'll come after ya. Tha's 'is money ya got. Ya carn' fuck with flesh an' blood.

RAY. e's shat on you all your life, ya silly cunt.

PETE. What da you fuckin' know, ya jus'one of our drummers.

RAY. Ours! I want ya ta remember something, we're goin' way back, so think clearly. The firs' drum we done, top floor. You trembled aroun' on the roof, while I passed the gear up to ya. An'it was summer s'don' say it was cold.

PETE. Put 'enry's reddies back on the table Ray.

RAY Do you remember that drum?

PETE. This can still be forgotten.

RAY. I said ah wouldn'kill ya an'I meant it, but ah'll definately cut ya. Now fuckin' remember.

PETE. Leave me family out o' this.

RAY *steps towards* PETE *ready to cut him.*

PETE. I remember it a'right.

RAY. Ah know ya do.

PETE. We 'id the gear in the lift shaft. An' it was fuckin' cold.

RAY. 'enry stood at the bottom of the stairs keepin' dog coz 'e's a wanker.

PETE. You won' be sayin' that tomorrow.

RAY. Then wot 'appened, Pete?

PETE. . . . Some cunt chored it . . .

RAY. Some cunt'll do, but ta be more precise, le's call 'im 'enry. Give the cunt a name.

PETE. 'enry would never do that!

RAY. I caught 'im. 'e gave me a score, tol'me not ta tell ya . . .

PETE. Ya lyin' . . . I can see it in ya face, ya fuckin' lyin' . . . I can see it.

RAY. I take it ya lost out then? Wot a fuckin' family.

RAY *walks over to the till.*

PETE You carnt talk!

RAY. A few beads short of a rosary the ole girl but I know where I stan'with 'er.

RAY *opens the till.*

Barry well . . . I ain'gotta clue . . . But you'd already infected 'im . . . Did ya think you could turn 'im into a wrong 'un like you an'enry an' nuffin' would come of it?

RAY *scrapes out what change there is and puts it in his pocket. He lifts up a pouch, shakes it. Satisfied, he drops in his bag.*

PETE. Ya carn' clear me out, fucksake Ray.

RAY *picks up his tin of tea and drops it in the bag, hangs the bag around his shoulder.*

PETE. Leave me something Ray.

PETE. Justa few quid . . . tha's all.

RAY. Ya know wot I'd do? I'd burn the fuckin'place down. But then you ain't me are ya? You would never 'ave the bottle to do that.

RAY *exits out of the right exit, we hear the street door open then close.*

PETE *starts to scrape more heroin from the table.*

Scene Three

ELLA *enters and walks towards her chair. She stops centre stage, turns and looks back towards the exit. Apprehensively* RAY *enters. He stops by the doorway and watches as* ELLA *drags a chair and places it beside hers. She stands aside to offer him the chair.* RAY *slowly walks across the stage and sits down.* ELLA *sits beside him. For a few moments they both seem at a loss for words . . .*

RAY. 'ave ya 'eard from Barry at all t'day?

ELLA No.

RAY 'e ain' phoned?

ELLA. I ain' seen 'im since yesterday afternoon . . . You look tired.

RAY. Yeh . . . I am . . . Ain' slept properly fo' twenny-two years.

ELLA. . . . I made your bed today . . .

RAY. I always said you was psychic, didn' I . . . ?

ELLA. I always know ya when ya due, Ray. Don't mean I'm psychic.

RAY. Wot about that time you said I robbed your work place?

ELLA. You did do it then?

RAY (*shrugs*). Yeh . . . Is that Mr Peters still there?

ELLA. Yeh.

RAY. I pissed on 'is seat.

ELLA. Tha's why 'e was so angry. God 'e was fumin' for days . . .

RAY. Then the place lit up an'the alarms went off. I only jus' got away.

ELLA. . . . Did Barry tell you I was nearly arrested?

RAY You?

ELLA Shopliftin'.

RAY Nahh.

ELLA. I 'adn' got Barry anything for Chris'mas yet, so I
picked up some socks. Then I changed my mind. Socks are
a bit obvious, d'ya think?

RAY. Can never 'ave enough socks.

ELLA. I was in the food section by then, so I just left 'em
be'ind the baked beans. The security guard came up to me,
Stood right in front of me, 'e did. They threatened me with
the police, searched my 'andbag, me pockets.

RAY. What shop was this . . . ?

ELLA. . . . It's different now. Different people . . .

Pause.

RAY. Why didn'you read my letter?

ELLA. . . . I put it away to read later. an' later . . . became . . .

RAY. It took me ages ta write.

ELLA. I don'know why I never read it, Ray . . . I've still got it,
I wouldn' ave thrown it away.

Silence. RAY *seems to be drifting away into sleep.* ELLA
stands.

ELLA. I'll go an'get the letter . . . ? I wanna read it, while
you're here . . .

RAY, *eyes closed, does not answer.* ELLA *exits.*

Silence.

ELLA *enters holding the letter. She stands looking down at*
RAY.

ELLA. Ray . . . Ray.

RAY. Sorry, Mum.

ELLA. Barry is alright en 'e Ray?

RAY. Yeh.

ELLA. 'e's bin 'angin' about with that Pete ya know.

RAY. I know . . .

ELLA. I don' think that Pete's ever liked you much.

RAY. I'm pretty certain.

ELLA. But Barry is alright?

RAY. When I las' see 'im, 'e was . . . I got something fo' you.

RAY *goes into his bag and pulls out the tea tin.* RAY *takes off the lid and hands* ELLA *the tin. She smells it.*

RAY What d'ya think?

ELLA Lovely.

RAY *hands her the lid, she puts it back on the tin, places it on the floor and sits in the seat beside* RAY. *She looks at the letter in her hands.*

RAY. You've got rid of your demons 'aven't ya, Mum?

ELLA. Not completely. Woss ya 'ostel like?

RAY Someone robbed me room the other day. Took me tape recorder. 'ad a CD on it an' everything. Remote control. I could sit on the bed an'change the stations on the radio.

Silence.

There's no buzz out there any more, Mum.

ELLA. Maybe it's time.

RAY. . . . I'm shattered . . .

ELLA. It's a' right. Sleep if ya wanna sleep.

RAY *does not answer and appears to already be asleep.* ELLA *opens the letter and starts reading it . . .* RAY *sleeps. Sirens sound in the distance.* ELLA *looks up . . .*

Blackout.

The end

A Nick Hern Book

Drummers first published in Great Britain in 1999
as a paperback original by Nick Hern Books Ltd,
14 Larden Road, London W3 7ST in association with
Out of Joint and the Ambassador Theatre Group, London

Drummers copyright © 1999 Simon Bennett

Simon Bennett has asserted his right to be identified as the
author of this work

Typeset by Country Setting, Kingsdown, Kent CT14 8ES
Printed and bound in Great Britain by Bath Press, Avon

ISBN 185459 457 5

A CIP catalogue record for this book is available from the
British Library